THE ROMANCE OF
ALEXANDER THE GREAT
BY PSEUDO-CALLISTHENES

Number LXXXII of the
Records of Civilization
Sources and Studies

**PSEUDO-CALLISTHENES. The Romance of Alexander the Great, tr.
with intro. by A. M. Wolohojian. Columbia, 1970 (c1969). 196p
bibl (Records of Civilization: Sources and Studies) 74-84593. 8.50**
The first English translation of a fifth-century Armenian version of the
Romance of Alexander the Great which was composed in Greek,
probably in Alexandria sometime before the fourth century A.D. by an
unknown author but falsely ascribed to Callisthenes, an historian contemporary with Alexander. The *Pseudo-Callisthenes*, as it was subsequently dubbed, became the main source of the vast body of lore and
legend which proliferated about the great conqueror during the Middle
Ages. Very little has survived of the original Greek text but the
Armenian version is apparently a very accurate rendering of the oldest
manuscript tradition and is therefore of great importance in recon-
structing the original. Translator Wolohojian (Rutgers) has supplied
the volume with a scholarly introduction, full notes, and an index.
This work will be welcomed by all students interested in the medieval
romances in general and the Alexander cycle in particular.

CHOICE   JUNE'70

*History, Geography &
Travel*

*Ancient (Incl.
Archaeology)*

PA
3946
C3
ES

Alexander crossing the Stranga

From Ms No. 424 in the Library of the Mechitarist Congregation, San Lazzaro, Venice.

THE ROMANCE OF
ALEXANDER THE GREAT
BY PSEUDO-CALLISTHENES

Translated from the Armenian Version
with an Introduction by
Albert Mugrdich Wolohojian

COLUMBIA UNIVERSITY PRESS
New York and London 1969

Albert Mugrdich Wolohojian is Associate Professor of Romance Languages at Rutgers—the State University of New Jersey, in New Brunswick.

Copyright © 1969 Columbia University Press
Standard Book Number 231-03297-8
Library of Congress Catalog Card Number: 74-84593
Printed in the United States of America

ACKNOWLEDGMENTS

THE PRESENT VOLUME developed from the work submitted in partial fulfillment of the Ph.D. degree at Columbia University in 1964. I am deeply indebted to Professor Lawton P. G Peckham, who encouraged the translation from the beginning and patiently saw it through its successive revisions. I also thank Professor W. T. H. Jackson of Columbia and Professor J. Undank of Rutgers University for their suggestions and comments.

I deeply regret that this acknowledgment of their interest and encouragement will not be seen by Professor Ben Edwin Perry of the University of Illinois, whose wide range of scholarly interests included Armenian letters, and Mr. Artin K. Shalian of New York, whose nobility of heart and mind is a shining memory.

This book is a tribute to the Mechitarist Fathers of Venice and their late abbot, my beloved uncle, Archbishop S. Oulouhodgian.

CONTENTS

THE ROMANCE OF
ALEXANDER THE GREAT
BY PSEUDO-CALLISTHENES

INTRODUCTION

O F THE MANY legends of antiquity that flourished again in the vernaculars of the Middle Ages, none caught the fancy of so many and so diverse peoples as the fantastic adventures of King Alexander of Macedon. By the seventeenth century, the fanciful biography of the Macedonian world conqueror had appeared in over eighty versions in twenty-four languages.[1]

It was, then, not historical accounts[2] that were to fascinate the popular imagination of the Middle Ages so much as the Romance composed probably in Alexandria sometime before the fourth century A.D. by an unknown author whom certain manuscripts falsely name Callisthenes, kin of Aristotle and companion and historian of Alexander the Great.[3] And it is this Romance designated subsequently as the *Pseudo-Callisthenes*, that, with its interpolations, redactions, and translations, is the source of most of the episodes of the Alexander stories that were to proliferate in the Middle Ages.[4]

[1] W. Schmid and O. Stählin, *Geschichte der griechischen Literatur* (Munich, 1924), II, 813 ff.

[2] It is somewhat arbitrary to separate the historical from the legendary tradition as contemporary records of Alexander have not survived and the historical tradition was not to be set until centuries after his death. By that time, history had been infused with the popular legends of the marvelous. A. Abel, *Le Roman d'Alexandre, Légendaire Médiéval* (Brussels, 1955), pp. 9-10.

[3] W. Kroll, *Historia Alexandri Magni* (Berlin, 1926), Introduction, p. xv. Certain manuscripts (late Beta, or *B*, group) name Callisthenes, while Valerius attributes the work to Aesop; the Armenian printed text, Venice ms. 424, notes at the end of the first major section that the work was written by Aristotle.

[4] P. Meyer, *Alexandre le Grand dans la littérature française du moyen âge* (Paris, 1886), Vol. II, ch. 1, states that medieval originality lies

Although the question of the classification of the surviving manuscripts of the *Pseudo-Callisthenes* has beguiled generations of scholars, it is generally agreed that the tradition closest to the lost original is best represented by manuscript No. 1711, *fonds grec* of the Bibliothèque Nationale (Paris), supplemented and corrected by the fifth-century Armenian translation, and the middle fourth-century rendition into Latin by Julius Valerius, which was to have such a rich and varied descendance in the literature of northwestern Europe.[5]

This group of texts is generally designated as the Alpha (or *A*) group; and to it belongs probably also an eleventh-century Arabic version. The majority of extant Greek manuscripts belong, however, to the Beta (or *B*) group, which developed from reworkings of the Alpha. The Gamma text group, which Müller[6] designated as C^1, is an expansion of *B*, with interpolations. A Syriac version is attributed to the Delta (*D*) group of which no Greek text survives. To it belong also an Ethiopian version and the lost Greek source used by Archpresbyter Leo of Naples for his tenth-century Latin translation, *Nativitas et Victoria Alexandri Magni*, or the *Historia de Preliis*, which became one of the most important lines of transmission into western medieval literature of the *Pseudo-Callisthenes*.

The editor of this text,[7] F. Pfister, has ranked it with the Armenian, the Syriac, and that of Valerius in its usefulness for the reconstruction of the lost Alexandrine original; and indeed, he suggests it may surpass all other texts in its fidelity to the earliest Greek text.[8] However, its brevity and sparseness, cited

---

in the addition of local color and the changes in the personality of the hero and that nearly all the episodes may be traced to antiquity.

[5] F. P. Magoun, Jr., *The Gests of King Alexander of Macedon* (Cambridge, Mass., 1929), pp. 22-62, reviews the development and diffusion of the *Pseudo-Callisthenes*.

[6] C. Müller, *Reliqua Arriani, et Scriptorum de rebus Alexandri Magni* (Paris, 1846), Introduction, pp. vii-x.

[7] F. Pfister, *Der Alexanderroman des Archipresbyters Leo* (Heidelberg, 1913). Pp. 40-41 give genealogical tables of the Romance.

[8] *Ibid.*, Foreword, p. v.

by Pfister to substantiate its antiquity, generally detract from its coherence and suggest, in fact, that the Greek source text used by Leo may have been an abridged version or that Leo saw fit to shorten it in the translating, frequently at the cost of intelligibility.

We shall see that the Armenian, by contrast, sustains a narrative coherence that is singular among surviving versions of the *Pseudo-Callisthenes*. Its textual fullness in comparison with Leo, rather than suggesting that the Armenian was based upon a late, extended, Greek original, seems to confirm its fidelity to an original which was in its narrative and its psychology a coherent whole. In brief substantiation of this, we can note the remarkable subtlety of the character delineation of Olympias and Nectanebos in the seduction sequence (Leo, Bk. I, ch. 4; Ar. chs. 6-9.) The Armenian presents in all its duplicity and concupiscence their voluntary and mutual deception. It could also be noted that Leo (ch. 18), fails to present a characterization of Nikalaos which naturally supports the subsequent exchange of hostilities with Alexander, while the Armenian (chs. 49-51) does. A further example is the failure of Leo (ch. 31b) to concern itself with Iollas' motives for entering into the conspiracy to poison Alexander, while the Armenian (chs. 262-66) presents with an engaging comprehension the bonds of perversion of the partners-in-regicide.

As evidences of the internal textual coherence of the Armenian, the following few episodes may be presented as noteworthy.

In Leo, chapter 3, the Egyptians write the royal prophecy on a stone and there is no further mention of it; whereas in the Armenian, chapter 4, it is written on the base of the statue of Nectanebos, where Alexander will read it in chapter 96 when he returns to Egypt in fulfillment of the prophecy.

Darius' death gives two further examples of textual coherence in the Armenian, which are not found in Leo. Thus the dying Darius will recall that Alexander has dined with him (ch. 196, referring back to ch. 180). In Leo, Book II, chapters 20-21, there is no warning by Darius to Alexander to be wary of his fellow countrymen, as in the Armenian, chapters 195-97. And thus an important parallel between the deaths of the two kings is lost. This warning will in fact anticipate the prophecy of the magic trees (Ar. ch. 209, and missing in Leo) that Alexander will be killed by his own men. It is evident that such passages in the text of the Armenian are in fact essential to the development of the narrative structure itself.

Besides the apparent lacunae of the Leo text, Book I, chapters 15-16, 25-28, 32; Book II, chapters 2, 22, there are many examples where the brevity of Leo causes obvious impoverishment of the text. Thus in Book I, chapter 8 (Ar. chs. 16-17), the symbols in Philip's dream concerning Olympias' conception are not adequately explained. In chapter 30 (Ar. ch. 77), there is only a mention of a prophecy from Ammon whereas the Armenian gives the verification by the god of his paternity of Alexander. Leo, Book I, chapter 36 (Ar. ch. 103) does not detail Darius' reasons for his choice of gifts to Alexander and thus loses the antithesis of Alexander's reply. Again there is no explanation in Leo, Book I, chapter 45 of the prophecy about Alexander Heracles (Ar. ch. 125). The incident of Stasagoras and the priestess is shortened in Leo to the point of incomprehensibility. Thus, too, in Book II, chapter 21 (Ar. chs. 200-2), Leo loses the clever play on Alexander's promise to make the murderers of Darius conspicuous among men.[9]

It must also be noted that the Armenian text is remarkably rich in references to Alexandria, which should further substantiate its fidelity to the lost original. In contrast to Leo, chapters 70 and 89 deal at length with the founding and establishing of Alexandria and in chapter 93 there is an eloquent tribute to the glory that will be Alexandria's. That the great glory of Alexan-

[9] By contrast, infrequent instances where Leo is more extensive than the Armenian include Bk. I, ch. 36 (Ar. ch. 103) where Darius is shown a picture of Alexander by the Tyrians before sending him his disdainful gifts. Also in Leo, Bk. I, ch. 40 (Ar. ch. 112) the interesting exchange of pepper and poppy seeds as symbols of force versus number is not in the Armenian. The Armenian also lacks the compassionate letter of Alexander to the Lacedemonians (Leo, Bk. II, ch. 6).

der will be inextricably bound to the glory of the city itself is a constant theme that further distinguishes the Armenian from Leo. In chapter 144, Demosthenes, himself, will give glowing praise to the Egyptian city; and in chapters 247-50, even the god Sesonchousis envies Alexander the immortality that is his for having founded the royal city that will forever bear his name.

Thus, if the Armenian version of the Alexander Romance was to have no great importance in the development of the legend in the East (unlike the lost Pehlevi which was the source of the seventh-century Syriac),[10] it is of prime importance in the reconstruction of the original text itself, as it appears to be an extraordinarily accurate rendering of the oldest manuscript tradition.[11]

An Armenian text was first published in 1842 by the Mechitarist Fathers of Venice,[12] and its importance has been noted by every student of the *Pseudo-Callisthenes* since Julius Zacher, its first serious critic.[13] Despite the avowed importance of the Armenian text, the scholars who turned their attention to the Armenian *Pseudo-Callisthenes* were few in number and handicapped by their lack of access to the Armenian language. Zacher,

---

[10] Th. Nöldeke, "Beiträge zur Geschichte des Alexanderromans," *Denkschriften der Kaiserlichen Akademie der Wissenschaften in Wien,* XXXVIII (Vienna, 1890), 1. The Armenian did, however, serve as the basis for a lost seventeenth-century translation into Turkish.

[11] Kroll, in the introduction to his reconstruction of the Alpha text, states: "Homo ille Armenius codicem A simillimum fideliter secutus est, ut sine eius opera multa codicis A damna sarcire omnino nequiremus; quamobrem ex hac versione plura excripsi quam ex ullo alio textus fonte." (Kroll's text has been translated by E. H. Haight, *The Life of Alexander of Macedon by Pseudo-Callisthenes* [New York, 1955].)

In a more recent study of sources, R. Merkelbach, "Die Quellen des griechischen Alexanderromans," *Zetemata,* IX (Munich, 1954), 64, states: "Die wichtigste der Übersetzungen ist Arm. Sie ist neben A unser bester Text und verbessert ihn an zahlreichen Stellen."

[12] R. T'reanç, ed., *The History of Alexander of Macedon* (Պատմութիւն Աղեքսանդրի Մակեդոնացւոյ) (Venice, 1842).

[13] J. Zacher, *Pseudo-Callisthenes, Forschungen zur Kritik und Geschichte der ältesten Aufzeichnung der Alexandersage* (Halle, 1867), pp. 85-101.

whose chapter on the Armenian text is the source of most subsequent commentary, also gives the substance of preceding studies.[14] From a few compared passages, he noted the great fidelity of the Armenian to a Greek text which surely related to the Alpha group. Despite its changes and corruptions, Zacher found that in many ways the Armenian was more complete and better preserved than even the Greek Alpha text or Julius Valerius.[15]

In 1886, Adolf Baumgartner published his work on Moses of Khoren (Movses Xorenaçi, Մովսէս Խորենացի), the "father" of Armenian history, to whom, as we shall see, the Armenian translation has been generally attributed; and he called attention to the passages which had been borrowed by this author from the Armenian *Pseudo-Callisthenes*. In the same year, Johann Gildemeister noted further borrowings of the same nature.[16]

The fact that even the great European Syriac and Arabic specialist Theodor Nöldeke[17] cited his dependence upon Zacher, Römheld, and Hübschmann for information on the Armenian text underlines the linguistic barrier that separated the Armenian *Pseudo-Callisthenes* from European scholarship until Richard Raabe in 1896 undertook to recreate in Greek the Armenian

[14] *Ibid.* The first mention of the Armenian text by R. Geier (in his *Alexandri M. Histor. Scriptores* [*Leipzig*, 1844], p. 1.) was cited by C. Müller, where the publication of the ms. and the general facts of attributed authorship, dates, etc., are noted as well as the divisions of the text, which Geier saw as corresponding to the Greek A and Valerius. This was followed by a brief article by an unknown author in *Hallische Allgemeine Literatur-Zeitung* (June, 1845), pp. 1027-1029. There was also an article by C. F. Neumann in *Gelehrte Anzeigen, herausg. von Mitgliedern der k. bayer. Akademie der Wissenschaften* (Munich, December, 1844), pp. 961-983; cited by Zacher, p. 88.

[15] This same view was shared by Römheld in "Beiträge zur Geschichte und Kritik der Alexandersage," *Jahresbericht über das königliche Gymnasium zu Hersfeld* (1873), pp. 3-52.

[16] A. Baumgartner, "Über das Buch 'die Chrie,'" *Zeitschrift der deutschen morgenländischen Gesellschaft* [hereafter referred to as ZDMG], XL (1886), 457-515; and J. Gildemeister, "Pseudocallisthenes bei Moses Von Khoren," *ZDMG*, XL (1886), 88-91.

[17] Nöldeke, pp. 1-2.

translation,[18] and thus make possible for the first time serious attempts to reconstruct the lost Greek original. Raabe was not concerned with the Armenian tradition of the text and its problems of authorship and manuscript classification. In its relationship to the Greek tradition both the importance and the limitations of his work were underscored by Adolf Ausfeld[19] who, while realizing the importance of a translation of the Armenian, felt that a much more useful service would have been rendered by a literal translation of the text. Wilhelm Kroll thought more highly of Raabe's work,[20] but agreed with Ausfeld on the importance of the Armenian text itself.[21]

Armenian scholarship on the subject has not been extensive. The first Armenian to study the text was Father Raphael T'reanç (*Թրեանց*) in his introduction to the published text.[22] In 1887, an article appeared in support of the already widely held hypothesis that the *Pseudo-Callisthenes* was the translation of Movses Xorenaçi. On the basis of the Venice printed text, Father Jacob Dashian of the Mechitarist Order of Vienna published, in 1892, a study of the Armenian *Pseudo-Callisthenes*, which is not only a survey of the history of Alexander in Armenian literature but also a valuable textual study enriched by Father Dashian's access to variant manuscripts in the Vienna Mechitarist library and information he was able to obtain on manuscripts in other collections.[23] In 1938, Father N. Akinian of Vienna promised a new edition of the Armenian *Pseudo-Callisthenes* based on a hitherto unedited pre-Keçaroweçi text which has not yet appeared.[24]

---

[18] R. Raabe, Ἱστορία Ἀλεξάνδρου: *Die armenische Übersetzung der sagenhaften Alexander Biographie (P-C) auf ihre mutmassliche Grundlage zurückgeführt* (Leipzig, 1896).

[19] A. Ausfeld, *Der griechische Alexanderroman* (Leipzig, 1907), pp. 12-14.

[20] Kroll, Introduction, p. viii.

[21] Ausfeld, p. 12, "An vielen Stellen bietet der armenische Text unter allen die beste Überlieferung."

[22] See above, footnote 12.

[23] J. Dashian, *Studies on Pseudo-Callisthenes' Life of Alexander* (*Ուսումնասիրութիւնք Սորյն Կալիսթենեայ Վարուց Աղեքսանդրի*), (Vienna, 1892).

[24] Father Akinian, "Die handschriftliche Überlieferung der arme-

Thus, the Venice 1842 edition and Dashian's study of it remain the primary materials for the study of the Armenian *Pseudo-Callisthenes*.

THE ARMENIAN PSEUDO-CALLISTHENES

Although it is true that Armenian literature of the fifth century, the Golden Age, is largely one of translations, these translations usually concerned themselves with Christian theological subjects. The existence, then, at this date of an Armenian *Pseudo-Callisthenes* is remarkable.[25] While many great rhetorical, philosophical, and poetic works of classical antiquity remained untouched by Armenian translators, the romantic legend of Alexander started a career in Armenian letters that was to flourish through subsequent centuries and the vestiges of which are still alive in popular myth and legend.[26]

Since, however, the oldest surviving Armenian manuscript of the *Pseudo-Callisthenes* dates from about the fourteenth century, it is natural to wonder about the changes it may have undergone in the centuries that separate it from the original translation. Favorable to the corruption of the manuscript could have been the fact that the essentially pagan spirit of the Alexander text must have been foreign to the monastic scribe who made the new edition of the work.

In the Notice that follows the translation, the copyist, a certain Xačatowr Kečaroweçi (Խաչատուր Կեչարուեցի), describes the text as "unseemly" and "baseless" "pagan writings."

---

nischen Übersetzung des Alexanderromans von Pseudo-Kallisthenes," *Byzantion*, XIII (1938), 206. There is a discussion of this text in J. Skinner, "The Alexander Romance in the Armenian Historians," unpublished Harvard University Ph. D. thesis (Cambridge, Mass., 1940).

[25] Akinian, in *Byzantion*, XIII (1938), 201. "Das einzige hellenische Geschichtswerk, das in die christlich-armenische Literatur übernommen wurde, ist der Alexanderroman."

[26] Minas Tcheraz, "La légende d'Alexandre le Grand chez les Arméniens," *Revue de l'histoire des religions*, XLIII-XLIV (1901), pp. 345-51, discusses interesting folk tales still alive in Armenia c. 1900.

He speaks of his work in rather ambiguous and much contested terms as consisting of the "concordance of these meager things" and in the "writing of these words." He states that the pagan writings were "lacking in unity" and "unseemly" and that the copy before him, although choice and from an old text, was still "unskillful" and faulty, and he claims that by "editing and correcting in a poetic fashion," he "cleared a straight path" through this material.[27]

A review of prior Armenian texts that draw upon the Armenian translation of the *Pseudo-Callisthenes* does much to help arrive at a clearer understanding of what must have been the nature of Kečaroweçi's "editing and correcting." Fortunately such passages appear very early, and the familiarity of many authors with this tale is apparent from the frequency of references, whether direct or indirect, that can be traced to it.[28] Such references are interesting testimony to the popularity of this pagan romance among Armenian Christian writers even though they may not be specific enough to substantiate the integrity of the thirteenth-century text iself. For such substantiation, it is necessary to look for verbatim passages that appear in early texts.

Thus, we find that Tovma Arcrowni,[29] the tenth-century

[27] T'reanç, p. 195, note 1.

[28] Dashian, pp. 24-34, cites many other pre-thirteenth-century writers who show familiarity with the *Pseudo-Callisthenes*. Among them, Mxit'ar Goš (*Մխիթար Գոշ*) in his *Datastanagirk'* (*Դատաստանագիրք*) (Vałaršapat, 1880), uses the same adjectives to describe the bullheaded horse of Alexander as does the text, while the Greek would normally have been rendered in Armenian as *գլախլուխ* - (βουκέφαλος). Thus, too, there are indirect references in the *History of Armenia* by Yovhan Catholicos (Moscow, 1853), and Nerses Šnorhali's *Vipasanowtiwn* (*Ճառագործութիւն Հովհերականն Վիպասանութեան*), (Venice, 1830), from which Dashian traces a description of Varazdat as a new Achilles to the Armenian *Pseudo-Callisthenes*. It is interesting to note that the incident of Alexander's asking for a feather to bring up his wine at the time of his poisoning appears in Grigor Magistros (Vienna, unpublished manuscript No. 50, p. 154), and is in the Armenian, Syriac, and Leo versions, but appears in neither *A*,*B*,*C*, or *L*.

[29] *The History of the Arcrowni Dynasty* (*Պատմութիւն Տանն Արծրունեաց*), (St. Petersburg, 1887).

9

historian, mentions the unknown country "Šaxrik'" (*Շախրիք*)
as reminding him of paradise and proceeds with a description
of it that coincides with that of a letter of Alexander to his
mother. There is also a practically verbatim parallel between
the Armenian *Pseudo-Callisthenes*, page 126, lines 9-16 of the
printed text and Arcrowni, page 29, lines 14-19. These similarities, then, in texts which are separated by at least three centuries
indicate that the Armenian *Pseudo-Callisthenes* had been trans-
mitted with remarkable fidelity to the original translation.

It is interesting also to observe that Arcrowni is not critical
of the tales that he recounts; but he interprets the story in a
Christian context, a pattern that Kečaroweçi will follow in turn
in the thirteenth century.

Arcrowni could serve as the touchstone to test the quality
of the surviving Armenian text. However, the real abundance of
references to it are found in the fifth-century *History* of Movses
Xorenaçi, a fact which not only helps confirm that the surviving
text is relatively unchanged but also leads to the probable conclusion that Xorenaçi himself was the translator of the work.[30]

[30] There has been extensive controversy on the dates of Xorenaçi
since the early nineteenth century when scholars began to challenge the
traditional fifth-century dating. The dispute reached its peak at the
turn of this century when there was considerable support for a seventh-
or eighth-century dating. The English Armenologist Frederick C.
Conybeare with a reversal of his previously held position was among
those who led the movement back to the original dating, which is now
once again generally accepted. The controversy is discussed in detail
by S. Malxasian, *The Armenian History of Movses Xorenaçi* (*Մովսէս
Խորենացի Հայոց Պատմութիւն*), (Erevan, 1961), pp. 53-58. Malxasian himself is convinced of the fifth-century dating. F. Feydit writes:
"Moïse de Khorène, enfin, que la critique de la fin du siècle dernier
s'est efforcée de repousser au VIIIᵉ, voire au IXᵉ siècles, . . . semble bien
finalement être, comme il le dit lui-même, un élève de saint Mesrob,"
Pazmaveb, IX-XII (1962), 283-89.

In any case, there is no controversy about the dating of the translation of the Armenian *Pseudo-Callisthenes* as even Father Akinian who
insists upon a ninth-century dating of Xorenaçi places the *Pseudo-
Callisthenes* in the fifth century since Łazar P'arpeçi used it in his *History*
written in 504.

10

The existence of parallels between the text of Xorenaçi and the *Pseudo-Callisthenes* has long been observed by critics. In 1836, the identical passages in the two works were noted by the editors of the *New Armenian Dictionary*,[31] and picked up and commented upon by Baumgartner,[32] thus surely refuting Gildemeister's statement that the Mechitarists had no reason other than stylistic to date the work in the fifth century.[33]

Dashian cites at length and in detail many correspondences, often verbatim, between Xorenaçi and the *Pseudo-Callisthenes*, and concludes that the Armenian *Pseudo-Callisthenes* served as a stylistic guide to Xorenaçi and that the copy he used was almost identical with the Kečaroweçi text.

Thus the *Pseudo-Callisthenes*' description of the episodes at Tyre and Thebes can be compared with Xorenaçi's description of the destruction of Tigranakert.[34] It is remarkable that this passage, one of the finest in Xorenaçi's work, is a verbatim borrowing from the fantastic Romance with those changes only that were essential to the new situation. The similarity of these passages has often been noted and had been suspected even from the days of Magistros.[35]

In the passage on the conquest of Tigranakert, Xorenaçi takes a whole chapter from Callisthenes' description of the siege

[31] Նոր Հայկազեան Բառարիրք (Venice, 1836), p. 18.

[32] See above, footnote 16.

[33] In ZDMG, XL (1886), 90. It is true that the editor of the 1842 edition relies most heavily on stylistic and linguistic supports for his attribution to Xorenaçi.

[34] Xorenaçi, Bk. III, chs. 26-28; vs. P-C, ch. 99.

[35] Gildemeister and Biwzandaci have so noted (Dashian, pp. 56-57); *Pazmaveb* has had two articles on this subject. One is by E. A. Sowk'rian, I (1878) 7-14, showing that Xorenaçi follows the fallacious Callisthenes to the point of parting from historical veracity. F. P. Sargsian, *Pazmaveb*, II (1883) 118-19, tried to show that while similarities are substantial, Xorenaçi has not falsified history. Sargsian suggests that the similarities might be accidental, especally since his text agreed with the history of Arrian, as well as the *Pseudo-Callisthenes*. Dashian insists, however (p. 60), that the cited passages show that although Xorenaçi has made slight changes, the use of the *Pseudo-Callisthenes* as his base is undeniable.

of Thebes.[36] As Gildemeister observed,[37] the additions that appear in Xorenaçi and which are also in the Greek must have been in the original Armenian text and have been subsequently lost in copying. To Gildemeister's contention that Xorenaçi has copied the Armenian translation, Dashian thus says it should be added that it was his own translation from which he was copying.

Even the earliest commentators on the Armenian *Pseudo-Callisthenes* were inclined to attribute the work to Movses Xorenaçi. Thus the editor of the Venice text,[38] Father Alishan,[39] and Father Sowk'rian,[40] who tried to substantiate the opinion that the *Pseudo-Callisthenes* was not only a work of Xorenaçi but one of his major works of translation, and that Xorenaçi, considering his translations as his own works, did not hesitate to draw upon them freely and without acknowledgment for his *History*.

There is likewise considerable uncertainty as to the date of the translation. The theories usually advanced are that it was done before or after his *History*,[41] when he was in Athens,[42] or that the translations were done in a group after the *History*.[43] On a linguistic basis, it even seems possible that it was translated in his youth in Alexandria.[44] Nevertheless, he does remark in the latter part of his *History* that "I am an old man, ill, and busy with my translations."[45]

The sequence of the borrowings from the *Pseudo-Callisthenes* in the works of Xorenaçi may be significant. Although he used it more than twenty times in his *History*, it is noteworthy that he never draws upon it in Book I, scarcely five times in

[36] Armenian *P-C*, chs. 126-27, p. 64; Xorenaçi, Bk. III, ch. 28, p. 214.
[37] *ZDMG*, XL (1886), 90-91.
[38] Introduction, pp. 7-8.
[39] *Pazmaveb* (1847), p. 153.
[40] *K'nnaser*, II (1887), 29-63.
[41] *Pazmaveb*, I (1878), 9.
[42] *Pazmaveb*, II (1883), 119.
[43] *K'nnaser*, II, 33, which however excepts the *Pseudo-Callisthenes* from this group and dates it prior to the *History*. (See Dashian, pp. 72-84 for discussion).
[44] Dashian, p. 73.
[45] *Ibid.*, p. 72.

Book II, and more than fifteen times in Book III.[46] The quotations from Book II are from early parts of the *Pseudo-Callisthenes*, while Book III draws from all parts (pp. 3-173) without distinction. Thus it seems logical to Dashian to conclude that Xorenaçi had not translated the Romance at the time of writing the first Book, that at about the time he was working on chapter 13 of Book II he started his translation and began to draw upon it as a historical source, and that he seems to have completed the translation by the beginning of the third Book. On this basis, despite considerable dissension as to the date of the *History*,[47]

[46] This is the way the borrowings appear (Dashian, pp. 73-74, note 1).

	Xorenaçi	Arm. Pseudo-Callisthenes
Book I	None	
Book II	33	39
	46	116
	62	31
	63	59
	79	32
Book III	8	51
	17	150
	19	122
	21	262
	26	92
	28	126
	32	58
	40	49
	47	3
	57	203
	58	71
	62	97

[47] There is no point in entering the lengthy disputes among textual critics of Xorenaçi on this subject. Suggested dates are: 480-483, *Handes Amsorea* (Հանդէս Ամսօրեայ), I (1887), 11; 486-490, *K'nnaser*, II (1887), 7-28, which dates the *Towkt* of Łazar P'arpeçi, c. 485, although these mention the death of Xorenaçi. It seems that Gildemeister is wrong (*ZDMG* [1886], p. 90) when, on the basis of Xorenaçi's use of the *P-C*, he dates it in the first half of the fifth century. Gutschmied (Encycl. Britt. XVI, p. 862) suggests a date of 634-642 for the *History* and questions its being the work of Xorenaçi. Baumgartner (*ZDMG*, XL [1886],

it seems to Dashian that the latest date for the *Pseudo-Callisthenes* translation should be c. 486.[48]

THE THIRTEENTH-CENTURY EDITION OF XAČATOWR KEČAROWEÇI

The thirteenth-century copyist, Kečaroweçi, Xačatowr of the monastery of Kečarowk, says, as we have seen, that although the copy he was working from was choice and old, it was "unskillful" and "corrupted" and adds that by "editing and correcting" it, he has "made a straight path." Yet it seems that the text as a whole is intact. Thus the question arises as to what precisely Kečaroweçi meant by these words.

There are two specific references to his own work; these two appear in only a few manuscripts and most manuscripts have neither. The first is in a Christian poem that is of little interest in the understanding of the text.[49] In the second, Kečaroweçi likens Alexander's deeds to those of Christ and tries to make of him a prototype of Christ. To the end of this poem, he attaches the Notice in which he pleads forgiveness for his audacity in making such a comparison. These remarks appear in the Kečaroweçi group of manuscripts and also those of a subsequent copyist, Zakariah[50] (Զաքարիայ).

Xačatowr Kečaroweçi, on the basis of his own words, was thought to have refashioned and changed the old Armenian text. Yet it has been seen that many extended passages can be traced intact to old authors and that in fact the thirteenth-century

---

505-6), says that the work, no doubt Xorenaçi's, dates after the *Geography* but before the *History*. Malxasian, p. 20, states that the *Geography* is now generally held to be the work of Anania Širakaçi (Անանիա Շիրակացի), and dates from the second half of the seventh century.

[48] Dashian, p. 76.

[49] T'reanç, ed., p. 195, note 2.

[50] Of the seventeen Arm. mss. controlled by Dashian, seven have neither piece of Kečaroweçi. Both pieces together appear only in Venice ms. 424.

author never betrays himself through the language of his own time in the body of the text. It seems clear that Kečaroweçi had no intention of rewriting the *Pseudo-Callisthenes* and his words should not be so construed.

The words "I worked faithfully at the writing of these words and the composing of these meager things" were meant probably for his own composition, in which he asks to be forgiven for having likened Alexander to Christ. "Meager things" would not refer to a new edition of the romance; and when he adds "I worked faithfully at the writing which I wrote with my own hand," he seems to be stating simply that he had copied the text and that he did not change it because it was "heathen" and "improper," but rather asks forgiveness, for his task was only the "copying of words," even if of a pagan spirit. There is, in Dashian's opinion, no other explanation for the retention in the *Pseudo-Callisthenes* of chapters 6, 17, or 26 "improper" parts, if any are; what is more, he composed poems on these parts.

There remain his last words "by editing and correcting" he made "a straight path." He may have had before him an earlier manuscript whose writing and spelling were "faulty" (անյարմար) and "corrupted" (շաղկապի) and these he had "edited and corrected." Finding his copy graceless and verbose, he wanted, by his poetic art (քերթողորէն), to transform it into a "straight path." He did this by writing an epigrammatic poem of his own after each section of the *Pseudo-Callisthenes*, taking his subject from the text itself. Certainly, Kečaroweçi added the preface and conclusion in which he tries to prove that if the snake of Moses, the trial of Joseph, and the contrition of David were prefigurations of the deeds of Christ, how much more so were the feats of the amazing Alexander. Perhaps this is that "pagan" and "improper" work for which he asks forgiveness.

Kečaroweçi also added a section of didactic poems on the death of Alexander, forms of which appear in all the manuscripts[51] and which the epitomes have in shortened form. These are Alexander's plaint at the time of his sickness, Olympias'

[51] Only 1601 has none. (Dashian, p. 106.)

15

lament at his death, followed by the lament of Roxiane, his generals, and his soldiers.[52]

These have all been attributed to Kečaroweçi, since in every manuscript they are followed by the remarks that the hearer of these poems should remember their composer, Xačatowr Kečaroweçi. Yet Dashian[53] remarks that Kečaroweçi's own style and language are too poor to allow these prosopopoeias to be attributed to him. It is significant that Zakariah and Grigoris of Ałt'amar (Գրիգորիս Աղթամարայ), in writing their own poems on the *Pseudo-Callisthenes*, after Kečaroweçi, treat the prosopopoeias as an integral part of the original text, and not as a later addition. Moreover, the single source of these laments is the Armenian translation of the *Pseudo-Callisthenes*. The author of these could be the same as the translator of the *Pseudo-Callisthenes*.

Although certain manuscripts are illustrated on almost every other page, unfamiliarity with the Armenian *Pseudo-Callisthenes* is seen in such a remark as that of Sir Wallis Budge,[54] who said, "Among the many peoples of the Near and Far East who have adopted Alexander as a fellow countryman, the Persians alone have attempted to illustrate their versions of his life . . . with pictures." Copies of these illuminations have appeared in Archag Tchobanian's *La Roseraie d'Arménie* (Paris, 1918-23); and they have been studied by Ferdinand Macler, *L'Enluminure arménienne profane* (Paris, 1928).

A subsequent copyist of the *Pseudo-Callisthenes*, Zakariah,

---

[52] Dashian, p. 112, notes that there is a fifth one whose authenticity has been questioned. In it Alexander exhorts his friends to works of charity and virtue. The mss. themselves include it not with the other prosopopoeias, but after the Notice. It seems to Dashian that the author of this work had before him a copy of Aristotle's work on Virtue to King Alexander, which was translated quite late into Armenian. This fifth account appears in Venice mss. 424, 1107, and 1489.

[53] Dashian, pp. 108-11, accepts Kečaroweçi's modest assessment of his own work. For a more recent judgment, see M. T. Avdalbegian, *Xačatowr Kečareçi* (Erivan, 1958) (in Armenian).

[54] E. A. Budge, *The Alexander Book in Ethiopia* (London, 1933), intro., p. 8.

16

Bishop of Gnunik', was perhaps of the same lineage as Kečaro-weçi.[55] From Zakariah's remark that his work was written in Rome and brought to Armenia to be presented to the priest Esayia (Եսայիա), it has been surmised that the reference is to Nčeçi, who lived at the end of the thirteenth century. This is unlikely as it would make Kečaroweçi contemporary to Zakariah, who claimed to be his descendant and eager to renew his glory.[56]

Zakariah is especially proud of his illustrations and from his work comes the inspiration for the paintings that decorate many copies of the Armenian *Pseudo-Callisthenes*. In certain manuscripts the poems that Zakariah adds to those of Kečaroweçi are indicated by marginal notes, but in others they are mixed together with no identifying notation. Even the notations are but a partial guide, however, as they too may have been miscopied.

Less important than this group of manuscripts are those of the Gregoris of Ałt'amar group. Gregoris was a sixteenth-century Catholicos;[57] from the manuscripts which contain his poems, it is not certain whether he made a new copy of the *Pseudo-Callis-thenes* or separately wrote poems which were later copied into the manuscript. He seems not to have touched the body of the work.

Dashian[58] has established that all the manuscripts he knew were based upon a lost Kečaroweçi original from which three groups of manuscripts have descended. The first group, which are full-length manuscripts, derives from a copy which was lacking chapters 132, 192, and 283 because of a loss of pages. A second group, the questionable, partially shortened manuscripts, stems from a copy lacking chapter 132. The third group comprises the Epitomes which come from a third copy missing

[55] On Zakariah, see N. Akinian, *Zakariah, Bishop of Gnunik, and his Poetry* (Vienna, 1910) (in Armenian).

[56] Dashian, pp. 124 ff. Akinian, in *Byzantion*, XIII (1938), 202 considers Zakariah Gregoris' pupil and dates him in the sixteenth century.

[57] On Gregoris, see N. Akinian, "Gregoris of Ałt'amar," *Handes Amsorya* (1914), pp. 18-63.

[58] Dashian, pp. 138-83.

chapter 192. Akinian has classified the thirty-two manuscripts known to him and gives the available bibliographical information on each.[59]

It is interesting to note that the questionable copies are sometimes more complete than the regular full-length ones and that the Epitomes, although written in a popular dialect and full of copying errors, often reveal a fidelity to *A* or Valerius greater than that of any surviving full-length copy.

In Venice there are ten manuscripts, seven of which are full length. The best of the full-length copies, which is undated, was used as the base text for the 1842 printing. It is a fine copy by a single copyist and is richly illustrated. It was traditionally accepted to be of the thirteenth century, but Dashian questions this dating as it is definitely of the Kečaroweçi group and is based, like all the full-length copies, on a single post-Kečaroweçi copy. There seems to be little doubt that the translation was made directly from a Greek manuscript in the fifth century. The translator had, in addition to a sound knowledge of the source language, the sensitivity to render the original into pure Armenian.[60] However, the translation dated from the Hellenophile second Mesropian school which tried to adapt Greek stylistic features into the Armenian, and the text often shows the marks of this effort. In addition, certain signs of the Greek original were ineffaceable no matter how careful the translator. Thus, for example, there are many plays on words, which Xorenaçi could not render literally, as indeed could not Valerius. Typical is the one where Alexander conquers Prince Nikolaos in a chariot race and the priest prophesies that as he conquered Nikolaos so too shall he conquer many peoples. The play on the proper name is lost as completely in Armenian as it would be in English.

The Greek stylistic influence may be seen in such non-Armenian constructions as the genitive absolute, the accusative

---

[59] N. Akinian, in *Byzantion*, XIII (1938), 203-5.

[60] Dashian strongly rejects a claim such as Ausfeld's (p. 13) "Mißverständnisse begegen ihm öfter, teils infolge seiner Beschränktheit teils wegen seiner mangelhaften Kenntnis der griechischen Sprache und der antiken Verhältnisse."

subject of an infinitive, plural subjects and singular verbs where the subject is neuter in the Greek, and in irregularities in the prefixed declensions. Yet these Greek forms were frequent in the Armenian style of the time and could even be found in the pure Mesropian style of the Golden Age.

It is often the custom of the Armenian to render proper names in the traditional Armenian manner, if such exists, thus Areg for πόλις τοῦ ἡλίου, and the gods' names: Anahit for Hera, Mir for Mithra, and the like. Yet in other places the Greek name is maintained often with the case ending.

These considerations do not detract from the fact that the translation, wherever verifiable, is identical to the original. Sometimes Xorenaçi's extreme fidelity to the Greek makes the text unintelligible in the Armenian.[61] But these instances are few, and in general the text is rich in old and essentially Armenian constructions; the English translation has followed, as closely as the archaic syntax and textual corruptions have permitted, the letter of the text.

For purposes of consistency in transliterating the Armenian, the phonetic equivalents of Professor A. Meillet[62] have been used for the purely Armenian names. In cases where a European spelling is already standard, as in the name of Dashian himself or the journal *Pazmaveb*, these spellings have been used. In the body of the text, it became apparent that the Armenian translator of the *Pseudo-Callisthenes* had not been consistent or systematic in the choice of Armenian letters to transliterate the Greek. However, the Transliteration Table below was arrived at, which in conjunction with Meillet's system, enabled a rendering of the Armenian names into standard Western equivalents. Thus such spellings as Kleovpatrē (Cleopatra) or Liwsias (Lysius) have been avoided. The Armenian is often extremely inconsistent in the spelling of proper names, confusing declined with nominative forms; in these instances a uniform nominative spelling has been

[61] Such as the riddle of *P*, ch. 45, lines 10-11.

[62] A. Meillet, *Altarmenisches Elementarbuch* (Heidelberg, 1913), pp. 8-9.

19

TRANSLITERATION TABLE

Armenian	Meillet	English
ա	ĕ	a or u
աւ	a	au or o
է	aw	e or ae
իւ	e	y
ղ	ł	l
կ	k	k or c
ով	ov	o
ու	ow	ou or u
ք	k'	k or kh
քս	k's	x

adopted.[63] Where the Armenian has translated the Greek into corresponding but not identical equivalents, as in the names of the gods, the Armenian has been rendered according to Meillet's system and the correspondence noted. In this way, despite the difficulties due to the nonsystematic transliteration of the original translator and subsequent textual corruptions, wherever possible standard Western forms of a proper name have been maintained.

Although there are of necessity references in the notes to the various Greek and Latin versions of the Romance, a comparative study of the *Pseudo-Callisthenes* has in no way been attempted. Certain interesting parallels, where a single Armenian paragraph corroborates readings from several different versions, have been cited as evidence of the antiquity of the Armenian and its apparent fidelity to a lost Alpha version more complete than any surviving Greek text of this tradition.

Finally, it should be noted that the Armenian printed text itself is extremely rare and referred to in an early Mechitarist catalog as "rarissime, essendone tirate pochissime copie."[64] There seem to be no copies in the principal libraries of the United States. This one text (Venice ms. 424) has been the basis of Western scholarship on the Armenian *Pseudo-Callisthenes* and has been regarded as the single most important source for re-

[63] See trans. note, 6.1.
[64] Zacher, p. 85.

20

establishing the badly corrupt Greek *A* tradition. There is little doubt that a new edition, based on the approximately forty extant Armenian manuscripts and drawing upon the passages surviving in old texts that have been subsequently lost in the Armenian *Pseudo-Callisthenes* would be invaluable for the study of the Greek tradition. Perhaps it is only fitting that obscure Armenian manuscripts should help clarify one day some of the mysteries that surround the origins of the Romance that, centuries after Alexander's death and disappearance, swept forth from the city that he founded to take the legend of the King of Kings into lands he did not dream of conquering and there, beyond the force of time and truth, brought him tribute that no earthly legions could exact.

A HISTORY OF THE GREAT WORLD CONQUEROR, ALEXANDER OF MACEDON 🦎

A LIFE OF BRAVERY AND HEROIC DEEDS AND, TOO, A DEATH MARKED WITH MARVELS

Aᴦᴛᴇʀ ᴛʜᴇʏ had determined the size of the earth and the sea and counted the stars of the sky, the wise men of the Egyptians imparted to the whole world power, the discovery and disposition of words, and the knowledge of practical skills. For it is said that the last king of Egypt, Nectanebos, after whom the kingdom fell from glory, conquered all men by magic sorcery;[1] even the natural elements obeyed him. For if ever a marauding horde rose against him, he did not work at machines of warfare, stockpile arms, prepare man-killing iron weapons, nor did he proffer any ingenious devices. Rather, he went to his palace alone, took a basin, and, isolating himself, worked this sorcery of the basin.[2] He poured spring water[3] into his basin, and with his hands created ships and men from wax, and set the men upon the ships and put them into the basin; and the men came to life.[4] And he, Nectanebos, took an ebony staff in his hand and by incantation invoked the gods of the earth and the spirits of the sky;[5] and in this fashion, he baptized the ships which were in the basin. As they were being baptized, the ships which were coming against them

1

by sea from their enemies were destroyed. And because of the masterful magic power of the man, his kingdom was at peace.

2 After much time had passed, certain men, who are called "exploratores"[1] by the Romans and scouts by the Armenians, came to Nectanebos and reported that a horde of soldiers had arrived. For the commander came to him and said: "Great king, set aside the festivities of peace and turn to war, for there is a great assemblage at hand. For not one nation comes upon us but many; the Indians, Kauanians, Koumenians, Oxydarkians, Eberians, Konians, Lelapians, the Bomtyrians, Argives, Azanians, and the Loukhalians,[2] and all the numberless nations that live in the East have reached Egypt with great armies. Recall the two Homeric verses; 'It is not fit nor proper that the wise man, to whom the people and so many cares have been entrusted, remain at sleep the whole night.' "[3]

3 And after the commander said this, Nectanebos smiled awhile and he said; "You spoke as was proper, which is fine; you are faithfully keeping your trust. However, you have spoken timorously and not as a soldier. For strength lies not in numbers but in the compulsion of desire; for one lion has caught many deer, and one wolf has harassed many flocks of sheep. So then, go with the soldiers assembled under your command and stand at your assigned watch; for with one word, I shall sink the barbarous hordes of countless nations in the waves of the sea."

4 Having said this, he dismissed the commander, and got up and went into the palace; and he ordered all those within to leave.[1] When he had isolated himself, he brought in the basin and set it down; and once again he performed the same act. Staring into the basin,[2] he saw the gods of the Egyptians and they were leading the ships of the oncoming enemies from the barbarous nations—he was a man who was accustomed to being among and speaking with the gods magically through his sorcerer's skill.[3] And upon learning that the kingdom of the Egyptians had come to

an end, he filled his belt with much gold and silver and shaved his hair and his beard. Having disguised himself, he fled away, without anyone's knowing, through Pellousion; and after traveling through many lands, came to the Macedonian city of Pella.[4] And clad in flaxen cloth,[5] he sat there practicing astrology as an Egyptian prophet, for he was really so skilled.

And when he was found not to be in the city, the Egyptians 5 beseeched their god and asked him what had become of the king. And he who was god in the underworld of Sinopos[1] delivered an oracle, speaking in this fashion: "That king of yours who fled will come again into Egypt, not having aged but rejuvenated. He will subdue your enemies the Persians." And when they had been given such an oracle by their gods, they sought to learn what these utterances could in fact mean. And they wrote them upon the pedestal beneath the statue of Nectanebos.

And in Macedon, Nectanebos became so famous to all by 6 examining the natural order, that even the queen, Olympias,[1] was to come and question him. For it happened in the time when Philip had left and gone to war. She ordered that the man be brought in to her for the examination of her affairs. And gladly coming in to see Olympias at her expressed wish, he stood stiffly before the queen without bowing; for he was pleasure-mad for women. He extended his hand and said, "Rejoice and be glad, Thou queen of the Macedonians"—he who was formerly the "Lord" did not think it fit to say "Lady."[2] And Olympias replied, "My joyful greetings upon you too, brave one; come, be seated." And when he had gone and sat down, she said to him: "Are 7 you the learned astrologer, Nectanebos, renowned in every city? Supposedly those who have interrogated you have learned every truth from you. By doing what kind of scientific study do you recount the truth?" And he said: "Queen, many are the researchers' ways[1] of examining; for there are dream tellers, omen solvers, dream judgers, the seers of Ammon,[2] basin gazers, birth readers, fortune tellers, fate tellers, who are called magi, and in their power rest all scientific matters." And having said this, he looked sharply at Olympias for he was smitten with lustful desire. Olympias, the queen, said, "Why did you stand stiffly upon seeing me?" He answered: "Royal lady, I remembered the oracle once made by my gods that I am to consult with a queen and investigate her affairs; and what I learned from their responses is true. So now, say what you wish."

8 And taking his hand out from beneath (his garment), he showed a tablet which no word nor effort can describe; for it was made of gold and ivory and showed seven stars: the ethereal astrologer, Aramazd, a sun of icy crystal, a moon of amaranthine, an Ares of hematite, an emerald Hermes, an Aphrodite of sapphire, and a Kronos of serpentine. And the horoscope was made of white marble.[1]

9 Olympias was amazed at the complex object and at the beautiful appearance of the stars. She came close to him and sat down and ordered all who were within to go out. She said to him: "Examine my birth and Philip's; for it is rumored that when he comes back from war, he is going to put me aside and take another wife." And he told her, "Set down your and Philip's birth sign." And she asked, "What is this you are doing?" Nectanebos set down also his own birth sign next to Olympias' and making his examination, said: "The rumor you have heard is not false. Yes, that is in fact destined for you. But as an Egyptian prophet, I am able to help you, so that you will not be put aside by him; and, even if you are, you shall find the one who shall avenge you." And Olympias said, "Is that true?" And he replied: "According to what you have presented me, you are destined to mate with an earthly god and to conceive from him; and after conceiving, to give birth and to nurse, and to have this (child) as your avenger of the wrongs which will come to you from Philip." "With which god?" asked Olympias, and he replied, "With the god of the Lybians, Ammon." Olympias went on, "How tall is he, is he young or middle-aged, and what is his physi-

cal appearance?" And he said: "He is white haired and has the horns of a ram above his jaws. Now then prepare yourself as a queen and a woman, for you shall see a dream concerning this and the god mated with you." And Olympias replied, "If I see the dream, I shall revere you not as a man but as a god."[1]

Nectanebos went forth from the palace and quickly picked and gathered a plant which he knew suitable for provoking dreams. And having rapidly done this, he made a female body of wax and wrote on the figure Olympias' name. Then he made a bed[1] of wax and put on it the statue he had made of Olympias. He lit a fire and poured thereon the broth of the plant, saying over it the vows suited for these doings, until the spirits appeared to Olympias; for he saw, from the signs there, Ammon united with her. And he rose and said, "My lady, you have conceived from me a boy child who shall be your avenger."   10

And when Olympias awoke from her sleep, she was amazed at the learned diviner, and she said: "I saw the dream and the god that you told me about, and now I wish to be united with him. Now let this be your concern; you should notify me at whatever hour he would mate with me, so that I might be found most ready for the bridegroom." And he said: "First of all, my lady, what you saw was a dream; but that very one who was the god in the dream is coming to unite with you. Allow me to sleep near you in the room, so that you be not afraid when the god is upon you."   11

And she said: "You have spoken wisely, Prophet. I shall give you access[1] to my room; and if I experience the mating and conceive, I shall greatly honor you as an infallible seer, and I shall receive you as though you were father of the child." Nectanebos said: "The first harbinger of the god who is coming to you is this: when you go inside and sit in your room, you shall see a serpent come slithering to you. You are to order those who are there to leave. Do not extinguish the light of the lamps, go and recline on   12 your couch and cover your face. Once again you shall see the god whom you saw come to you in your dreams." Having thus spoken, he left.

13 And immediately she gave him another room there close to her chamber. And he prepared the softest fleece of a ram together with the horns from its head, and a staff and a white robe. And he made a serpent, and he made it soft and limp; and it slithered out of his hands. All of a sudden he set the serpent loose and it entered Olympias' bedroom. And when she saw it, she was not afraid, for she had been expecting it. And she bid those who were there to go away, each to his own place. And she reclined on the bed and covered her face; only out of the corner of her eye did she see him assuming the appearance which she saw in the dream. And he put aside the date-tree wood staff, got up onto the bed and turned Olympias toward him and mated with her. Then he put his right hand upon her side and said: "Invincible and indomitable child. Long may you live, my lady, for you are pregnant with a boy child who shall be your avenger and become world conquering king[1] of the whole civilized universe." And having said this, he took his staff and left the room; and he hid the things he had.

14 And when it was morning, Olympias arose and came to Nectanebos' room. Awakening, he asked: "My lady, what is it? Tell me; did your dream come true?" Olympias replied, "Your words came true." And he said, "I rejoice with you, my lady." And Olympias asked: "Now is he not again to come to me? I await as a wife his coming and mating with me; for I received him with loving desire, Prophet. But I am surprised if this happened without your knowing, and you were not aware of it." And he rejoiced for he was loved by the queen. He said: "Listen, Olympias, I am the prophet of this god. If you will let me sleep here so that no one is disturbed or upset, I shall do the customary ablution for him and he will come to you." And Olympias said, "Let your will be done hereafter." And she said to her doorkeepers, "Give him the key to that room." And

28

when he acted, he did so secretly; and indeed he came to her as many times as Olympias desired that he come to her. Ahead of time, she let her wishes be known through the prophet, and he, as was his custom, mated with Olympias, giving the illusion that he was Ammon.

Her stomach was swelling, and she asked, "Prophet, what 15 shall I do if Philip comes and finds me pregnant?" And he said: "Be not afraid, my lady, for the god Ammon is helping you in this matter; he will come to him in a dream, and inform him of what was destined to happen. And you are to be unreproached and unpunished by him." Now depraved Olympias carried on in this fashion, revealing her true nature through the force of magic.

And Nectanebos made a sea falcon and bewitched it. And 16 as quickly as he wished, he saw Philip in his dreams. And exercising his magic on the falcon, he spoke, and caused the falcon to fly. And having flown over land and sea, in two days and two nights it reached the place where Philip was (and spoke to him in a) dream (as he had been taught by Nectanebos. Upon seeing the dream),[1] Philip woke up troubled; and he summoned Babylonios,[2] the reader of dreams, and said to him: "I saw, in a dream, a handsome white-haired god with the horns of a ram in his beard above his jaws. And he came in the night to my wife Olympias and lay with her. And upon rising, he said to her, 'You have conceived from me a boy child who shall fructify you and shall avenge his father's death.' And I seemed to patch up the womb of my wife with papyrus and to seal it with my seal. And the ring was of gold and the insignia, sunlike, with the head of a lion[3] and a lance. And this is what I thought I had done when the falcon came to me and awoke me from my sleep with his wings and gave no sign."

The dream reader said to him: "The dream that you saw is 17 true, since your sealing the womb of your wife is a proof-laden oracle. For the seal is proof, indicating that your wife has become pregnant, for no one seals an empty vessel but rather a full and loaded one; and this, with papyrus. Since

29

papyrus is found nowhere else but in Egypt, the man is Egyptian. And the seed is not vile but distinguished and glorious and radiant, especially because of the gold; for what is more glorious than gold, with which the gods are honored. And as the seal showed the sun and had a head of a lion and lances, he who is begotten shall reach as far as the East, and act in every matter just as he pleases according to his desires, like a lion. And he shall spear down peoples and cities on account of the spear that is in the dream. As for your seeing the horned hoary god, he was the god of the Libyans, Ammon."

18   When the interpreter of dreams had finished this explanation, Philip did not docilely hear of the pregnancy of his wife, even though he knew it was by the gods.[1] And having won the war, he rushed back to Macedon. Meanwhile, Olympias was afraid, and Nectanebos comforted her.

19   And when Philip returned and went to the queen, Olympias came to him, but, on account of the above happenings, not confidently. Upon seeing her troubled, Philip said: "My lady, you are not the cause of these things, for others are to blame; and what happened was pointed out to me in a dream so that you might be innocent and blameless. For we kings are able to do all things, but we can do nothing against the gods. For you were not smitten by any common vulgar man; nor was anyone cheaply covetous of your beauteous form; rather, it was the gods, who are all powerful." By having said this, he sent Olympias away in a happy frame of mind. And she was grateful to the forewarning prophet. And thereafter Philip was with Olympias.

20   Meanwhile Nectanebos was there in the palace, but did not appear to anyone since he did not wish to. But he heard Philip saying, "You were not made pregnant by the gods, but, in fact, were smitten by someone else whom I shall send forth from this life with pitiless tortures if he falls into my hands." And Nectanebos heard what was being said.

21   And while they were celebrating the king's return, only the

30

king was sad, because of his wife's becoming pregnant. And while the crowd was in merriment, Nectanebos transformed himself into the form of a serpent much bigger than the first. He passed through the palace breathing so fiercely that even the foundations quivered. And those who saw him fled away, startled and shaken by fear. Olympias recognizing her bridegroom was stunned and raised her right hand from her lap and extended it. And he circled the room, and then came to Olympias' knees, and flicked out his double-forked tongue and kissed her. The serpent thus, with positive proof, showed the spectators his loving embrace. But Philip was both frightened and amazed, and revealed his unawareness of its coming. And since Nectanebos did not wish to be seen too much by the audience, he transformed himself from the serpent into an eagle and flew away from there. As to where he went, it is unnecessary for me to say.[1]

But Philip had been terribly frightened. When he regained his composure, he said: "My lady, as sure proof, I saw the god come to help you in your peril. But, as to who the god was, I did not know, for he showed us the forms of Aramazd and of Ammon." Olympias said, "As he revealed himself to me at the time of mating with me, he is Ammon, the god of all the Libyans." And when the king heard this, he considered himself blessed for "I am destined," he said, "to be the father of a child of a god."

And a few days later, Philip had gone and sat in a grove in the palace where there were many birds feeding. Suddenly, while he was busy with important affairs, a bird came and laid an egg on his lap and flew away. And the egg rolled from his lap to the ground and broke open. From it a little serpent came forth and circled it many times. Then, wanting to go back into the egg from which it emerged, it struck its head on the way in and died instantly.

And since Philip was much[1] troubled, he sent for Antiphonta,[2] who was a celebrated omen teller of that time. And he told him the omen that had occurred: the bird, the egg, the serpent, its circling, its death. And Antiphonta, because special information had been inspired in him by the will of the god, said: "O King, you will have a son who, having traversed the whole world, shall subdue everyone by his strength and shall be subdued by no one; and while returning to his country, he shall die, having lived but for a short time. For the serpent is a royal animal, and the egg from which the serpent emerged, like the whole world. And when it had encircled the world and wanted to enter again the place from which it had emerged, it failed to do so and died." The man interpreted the omen in this fashion and related it to him; and upon receiving presents from Philip, he departed.

25 And when the fixed birth span of nine months for the completion of the pregnancy had come to an end, Olympias went and sat on the child-bearing throne to give birth. And Nectanebos stood close by, measuring the heavenly position of the stars. And by directing the disturbed natural elements by his own power, he learned that the time was not right[1] and he said: "Control and restrain yourself, my lady, for the present time and be like the person who gave you birth. For if you give birth now, your offspring will be born in servitude or as a slave to others."

26 When the woman was again impatient about having the child, for her many pains were unbearable, Nectanebos said, "Be patient a little longer, Queen, for if you give birth now, your offspring will be castrated or deformed."[1] And Nectanebos comforted the woman with consoling words; and he put his hand on her natural passageways and learned what was needed. And Nectanebos, with his power, prevented the birth. He looked again into the heavenly stars at the position of the natural elements, and he recognized that the whole universe was in harmony and that Kronos had come into the middle of the sky. He saw a bolt of lightning in the sky at noon, caused by the power of the sun; and he said to Olympias, "Give forth the cry of childbirth." And he himself delivered her child and said, "If you

give birth now, O Queen, the one you bear is a world conqueror." And Olympias cried out louder than a bull and gave birth to a boy child.

And when the boy fell to earth, there was an earthquake   27
and thundering; and frequent lightning flashes appeared on the earth, while nearly the whole world trembled. And Philip said: "I do not wish to rear that one, my lady, for he is not my offspring. But since I see that your seed is from the gods and that your birthgiving was accompanied by the omen of elemental occurrences, I shall rear him in the memory of my child who died, the one who had been born to me from my first wife; and he shall be called Alexander." Because Philip spoke in this fashion, the child received proper care; and there were crowning festivities throughout Macedon, Pella, Thrace, and throughout the nations.

And so as not to linger very long on the matters which   28
concern the rearing of Alexander, I shall start from the beginning to tell of the attentions he received. For when he was weaned and developed in size and shape, he did not resemble in the least Philip and Olympias, and not even his father; but rather, he developed features of a singular type. For he had the hair of a lion and one eye was blue; the right one was heavy lidded and black, and the left one was blue; and his teeth were as sharp as fangs, and he looked upon a defensive attack the same as a lion would. And his personality very clearly indicated what the boy would be like.[1] And in time he grew up and tried his wings at learning and at ruling.

His governess was Lakrine,[1] the Celt, sister of Melanos;   29
and his pedagogue and tutor was Leuonides, the Lakonian. The teacher of songs, Polinicos; and of music, Leucippos, the Lemnian; of geometry, Menechmos, the Peloponnesian; of rhetoric, Anaximenos Aristocles, the Lamphsakenian[2]; and of philosophy, Aristotle of Nicomitachos, the Stagirite[3] from the city of Meliteos. But Paphovranos mentioned   *Favorinus* these matters in the fourth book of his all-encompassing learned histories.[4]

33

30   And Alexander became learned in every matter and trained himself so well, as I said before, that it became clearly evident that he was being taught by some divinity. When he was free from tutorial counseling, from time to time he umpired his fellow students. And when he saw a team being defeated, he joined in the battle, and then, in turn, it was victorious. Thus it was clear that the victory was of his doing.

31   And at that time, the stablers came[1] and brought to Philip from his stables a huge, powerful horse.[2] And they brought it and stood it before him and addressed him in this fashion. "Lord King, we found this (creature), who is more beautiful and faster than Pegasus[3] or than Arion, born in your stables, and we have brought him from Lamomentios and we offer him to you." He was very surprised at seeing such great beauty and size, and said, "I swear by my salvation that he is beautiful."[4] "However, Lord," they said, "he is a man-eater." And he observed: "It is true that such things have happened among the Hellenes.[5] For he received a nature that was disposed to good and evil. Now since he has become evil, take him away and shut him up in a cell; bridle him[6] and imprison him so that we may throw before him anyone who, captured for a crime or a murder, falls under the laws of punishment." Once the king had spoken, the action was faster than the words.

32   Meanwhile, Alexander was growing and maturing. When he was twelve years old, he began to work with his father. He armed himself and went forth with the troops, and he liked to ride on horseback. And he saw that Philip was not on good terms with Olympias. Olympias had called Nectanebos to her and said, "Find out what Philip is thinking about me." When he had investigated, he came and sat down with her. And Alexander asked, "Father, are those heavenly stars which you are now talking about visible?" "Surely, son," he replied. "Can I, too, see them?" and he said, "You may, son."

33   And when it was night, he took the child out of the city,

34

and looked up into the sky and showed Alexander the stars. And Alexander seized him and took and threw him down into a pit. And he suffered severe blows on the neck in falling, and he said, "Alexander, my child, why did you want to do that?" And he replied, "Blame yourself, Astrologer." And he asked, "Why?" "For," he replied, "while not knowing the earth, you seek to study the affairs of the heavens." And he said: "I am dying, Alexander, for I suffered grievous harm in falling. But nothing and no mortal person can conquer fate." And the child asked, "Why?" And he replied: "I know how they had apportioned my life,[1] for it was written that I was to be slain by my son. And I was not able to escape this lot, but have been slain by you." And Alexander asked, "Am I then your child?" And he replied, "Indeed." "Really?" asked Alexander. "That is true," replied Nectanebos; and thus he told him of the flight from Egypt, the coming to Olympias, the inquiry into the stars, his desire, and how "I went to her as my god and I mated with her." Saying this, Nectanebos spat forth his spirit.

And upon learning that it was his father who had died, 34 Alexander was afraid to leave him in the pit lest he be eaten by wild beasts, for it was night and the place was desolate. Moved by compassion and pity for his sire,[1] he lifted him tenderly and bore him nobly on his shoulders within the gates. And coming before his mother, he told her everything that he had heard from the astrologer-magician. And Olympias was astonished and amazed; and she reproached herself, for, misled by deceptive and ingenious magic, she had committed adultery. Then she buried him, that very Nectanebos, as befitted the father of her child. She prepared a grave, and put him there.

It is astonishing to consider the destiny of Nectanebos. For 35 the Egyptian came to Macedon and was shrouded and buried in the Greek fashion. While Alexander, who was Macedonian, came to Egypt and had a native burial befitting a god.[1]

36 Meanwhile, after Philip had returned to his land and entered his palace, he sent to Delphi to get an oracle as to who would rule after him. And the oracle of Delphi, after drinking from the Castelian river of the underworld, spoke to him thus: "Philip, he who mounts the bullheaded horse and rides through Hellas[1] shall rule over the whole world and subdue all men with his spear." And that horse was called bullheaded because he had on his thigh an unusual scar which had the shape of a steer. And when the king heard the oracle, he was ever watching for a new Heracles.

37 And Alexander educated himself only with Aristotle, the Stagirite.[1] And as there were many children at Aristotle's for their education, and of these many were the sons of kings, the philosopher said to one of them, "If you inherit your father's kingdom, what will you give your teacher?" And he replied, "You shall live with me; and I shall appoint you co-ruler of my glorious kingdom." And he asked another, "And you, son, what will you do?" And he said, "I shall make you my administrator, and I shall appoint you advisor of matters to be judged by me." Questioning Alexander, he said, "If you rule the fatherland of the Macedonians, what will you do?" And he was silent a long while; then he looked at his teacher and said: "When you have no assurance of tomorrow, do you really seek to learn what is to be? Then shall I give what I shall pick and choose when Providence above decrees the time, hour and promise to be given." And when Aristotle heard this, he said to Alexander, "Hail, world conqueror, for you are destined to be a great emperor."

38 And now Alexander was loved by all as a keen-witted, intelligent, and gifted warrior. But Philip was of two minds. For he rejoiced in seeing such a warring spirit in his son, but was saddened at seeing that he did not look like him. Meanwhile Alexander distributed as gifts to others many things which he had been sent by his father.

39 And Zeuxis wrote a letter which said: "Greetings to Philip and Olympias, my lords; and information from your serv-

ant, Zeuxis, as to what Alexander is doing. What you are sending him is not adequate because he gives away so many gifts. Now you judge and decide what you deem proper to send me. I bid you farewell."

And they, in turn, wrote to Aristotle, his teacher, a letter   40 which went thus: "Philip and Olympias greet Aristotle, the teacher. Zeuxis, whom we have charged with the care of this boy, notified us that whatever we send to you is not sufficient for Alexander because he wants to give away many gifts. Now that you have found out about it,[1] set things right and notify us."

In answer, the philosopher wrote a letter that went like   41 this: "Aristotle, the teacher, greets Philip and Olympias. I do not think that it is I who advise your son to act in a manner foreign to his own and my and your customs. For I hear about and see his wisdom in acting with critical discernment; and he is able to judge and choose not as a youth but as an experienced man. Now do what you want to. Farewell."

And when they read this, they sent the following letter to   42 Zeuxis. "Philip and Olympias greet our dear Zeuxis. We sent Aristotle, the teacher, the letter you wrote us, so that when you receive this answer of his, you might try to set things right. Farewell."

Meanwhile, Aristotle was vexed and wrote reprovingly in   43 this fashion: "Aristotle greets his son, Alexander. Your parents wrote me that the allowance sent you by them is not sufficient for you, who, I think, would do nothing outside your own or my or your parents' wishes. Farewell, sweet child."

In return, Alexander wrote thus: "Alexander greets you,   44 my greatly gifted teacher, Aristotle. Know, father, that my allowance sent by my parents is unsuitable; however, it was right and proper to get angry upon hearing such things about their child. But now they have wronged me.[1] Farewell."

And likewise, his parents wrote Alexander a letter that let   45 him know about their wishes; and it went thus: "Philip and Olympias greet their son, Alexander. Take into consideration the honor of Philip and Olympias and do not scorn and reject the set allowance we send you, and do not scorn Aristotle's letter either. Instead, behave as befits you, and bear in mind other good thoughts. Farewell for us, dear and wise son."

46 In answer, Alexander wrote them a letter which gave them the following information. "Alexander greets Philip and Olympias. My fixed allowance, which you gave me through Zeuxis, is not worthy of Alexander, nor as befits Philip and Olympias to dispense. I do in fact bear in mind the counsel of my teacher, Aristotle, and I esteem that educator; but I reproach you for readily lending an ear to others, who are frequently depraved men and charlatans, yet remaining silent about such other matters which are natural obligations toward children, such as pertain to showing solicitude and care that would benefit me. I sincerely bid you farewell."

47 And when Alexander reached fourteen years of age, he happened to pass the place where the bullheaded horse was put away in a cell. He heard terrible neighing, and turning aside, Philip's son said: "What is this noise? Is it the neighing of a horse or the cry of a lion? Ptlomeos, who was afterwards called the Savior, was following him and he said, "Lord, this is the bullheaded horse which your father locked up and shut away for it is a man-eater." When the horse heard Alexander's voice, he neighed a second time, not a terrible and frightening outcry, but sweet, pleasant, and gentle. It seems to me the bullheaded horse was commanded by a god to act thus with Alexander. His whole mien was calm and clear as he started forward; and how gentle was the suppliant manner he showed his master.

48 And when Alexander saw his new mien, and noticed the traces of the many men who had been put to death, he, as a man, felt pity. And he elbowed aside the guards and opened the grated doors of the cage. Trusting in his ances-

try, he grabbed the halter of the horse and subdued him by physical strength rather than by luck, and he mounted him without a bridle. And immediately, someone ran off and recounted this to Philip. And he, recalling and remembering what had happened concerning this, went forth to meet his son. And he greeted him, saying, "Hail, Alexander, conqueror of the world." And Philip remained cheerful and happy in the secret and hidden hope for his son. And one day when Alexander was fifteen years old, he 49 found his father at leisure, and he embraced him and said, "Father, I beg you to permit me to go by boat to Pisa."[1] Philip asked, "Do you wish to see the Olympic contest?" The youth replied, "No, father; I want to take part in the contest." He questioned: "And in what sport have you been trained so that you would try to do it? For I know that as the son of a king, you know nothing more than to take part in the war-horse exercises. You do not know how to fight nor wrestle, nor any other discipline." Alexander replied, "I wish to drive a chariot, father." He said: "I shall see; let horses from my stables be prepared for you and let them be brought immediately to you, and you concern yourself in a praiseworthy fashion with the care of training them." He replied: "Just give me permission to go. I have my own horse which I have trained from the time he was young and I have raised him for myself." And he embraced him and was amazed at his eagerness; and he said, "Son, if you so wish, go."

And when he heard that he was going, he took the re- 50 sponsibility upon himself of ordering that a brand new ship be prepared and that the horses and chariots be put aboard. And sailing with Hephestion, his friend, he easily reached Pisa.[1] And he went out and took lodgings after ordering the servants to exercise the horses frequently and to work them hard. And he went off to stroll with Hephestion. And he happened upon a man whose name was Nikolaos. 51 He was a man of perfect stature, the king of the Akarnanians; and he was inflamed with the greatness of his possessions and with his good luck, two wavering gods; and he put his trust in bodily strength. He approached Alexander and greeted him at once, saying, "Greetings and welcome, young man." And he replied, "Greetings to you, too, whoever you are and from wherever you may be." And he asked: "To whom indeed do you think you are talking? My name is Nikolaos, king of the Akarnanians." And Alexander said: "Don't be so arrogant, Nikolaos, about the glory of your kingship, nor deem ephemeral things sufficient. For good luck does not come and stand firm in one place; but the tides of change shift always, and we have to accept strange things." And the other said to him: "You said that very nicely. But why have you come here? For I recognize that you are the son of Philip of Macedon." And he replied, "I have not come here to participate in the horse-riding contest, for I am still a boy; and not in the two-horsed chariots and in no other such contest." "Then," asked Nikolaos, "what do you want?" "I wish to drive a chariot." Nikolaos, bilious with rage, scorned his size not knowing the mettle of his spirit. He spat at him and said, "May no good come to you, nasty[1] little boy." And since he was well counseled and disciplined, he patiently refrained from an instinctive act and wiped off the saliva he had received from the enemy. And giving him a deadly smile, he said: "Nikolaos, I swear to you by my foolish father and the wonderful womb of the mother who bore me[2] that I shall conquer you here with the chariot and, in the land of the Akarnanians, I shall devastate you with my spear." And they parted from one another, with spirits heated for battle.

52 And a few days later came the time set for the contest. Nine charioteers entered, of whom four were sons of kings: that very same Nikolaos, Xanthias, the Boeotian, Kimon the Corinthian, and Alexander himself. The others were sons of generals and of satraps. The urn was placed; the trumpeters present apportioned the lots. First came Nikolaos; second, Xanthias; third, Kimon the Corinthian; fourth,

Klitomachos, the Balkan; fifth, Aristippos, the Olynthian; sixth, Pieros, the Phokoean; seventh, Kimon the Laconian; eighth, Alexander, the Macedonian; ninth, Nicomachos, the Lokrian. They took their positions on the race track, each upon his chariot.

The trumpet sounded the call to contest. The gate was 53 opened. They all rushed forth, and with a fearful charge sped through the first lap, the second, the third, and the fourth. And when the horses had been readied and had taken their positions, Alexander was the fourth charioteer. Behind him was Nikolaos, who was not thinking so much of winning as of slaying Alexander, for the father of Nikolaos had been killed in war by Philip.

Since keen-witted Alexander knew this, when those riding 54 ahead fell to the ground, Alexander let Nikolaos pass ahead; and, not realizing the cunning trap, he gladly passed in front thinking he was to be crowned victor. And he stayed ahead for two laps at which point Nikolaos' right horse stumbled and the whole chariot, together with the charioteer, collapsed in a heap. And Alexander savagely attacked him with the charge of his horses, and Nikolaos perished. Alexander continued on. And there was a saying about his dying that goes thus: He who plots evil for another does it to himself; and a bad thought is very bad for the thinker.[1]

And after Alexander had triumphed, he went to Olympian 55 Aramazd to be crowned with a crown made of a wild olive[1] bough. And the guardian of the shrine of Aramazd said to him: "Olympian Aramazd first of all tells you this, Alexander: that just as you conquered Nikolaos, so shall you conquer many people by war."[2]

And thus, after Alexander had slain Nikolaos and had re- 56 ceived a crown and superb honors worthy of a god, the conqueror went on to Macedon. He found his mother cast out by Philip; for he had taken in marriage as his wife his sister, Cleopatra, the daughter of Attanos.[1]

And on the very same day that the wedding celebrations 57

were taking place, he entered the dining hall with the Olympian crown on his head and said: "Father, accept my first crown of victory. And when I give my mother as bride to some king, I shall call you to Olympias' wedding." Having said this, he went and sat before the king. But Philip was disturbed over the words that had been spoken. And a certain man named Lysius, who was a parasite of Philip's, a dinner clown, a jester, was sitting there, and he said to Philip: "Now that your and Cleopatra your wife's wedding is taking place, may you who are mighty in all cities have from her truly legitimate sons similar to you in appearance."

58 And when Alexander heard this, he became angry; and he threw the goblet that he was holding and struck the buffoon's head and slew him. Seeing this, Philip stood up armed with a sword, and leaped at Alexander. But he struck his foot and stumbled upon the couch. When Alexander saw this, he remarked that he who had sped to take Asia and had captured all of Europe was not able to jump over the couch. Saying this, he snatched the sword away from his father and almost mortally wounded all those sitting there.

59 And before you, were to be seen the battles of the Lapiths and the Centaurs, and the things that happened because of the wedding of Perithias.[1] For some of them crawled under the throne; and some danced[2] with tables as though they were weapons; and others headed into dark places and fell. And there was a new Odysseus to be seen there as he went forth slaying Penelope's lovers; and he took his mother, whom he had avenged for the wedding festivities, inside; and his soldiers lifted Philip and lay him on the royal couch, performing their final duties.[3]

60 And days later, Alexander went in to him and sitting near him said: "Philip, I shall call you by your name lest it seem hard for you to be called father by me; for I have come to you not as your son, but as a friend to intercede in these things you have done. Now tell me this: Did Alexander do

42

right in slaying Lysius for his unseemly words? And did
you act rightly in attacking your own son, Alexander, and
wanting to kill him? And also, in wanting to take another
to wife, even though you were denied nothing by your
former wife, Olympias? Now stand up and behave like
yourself; for I know why you are feigning sickness. You
are suffering not physically but spiritually for your sins.
Now I beseech you to reconcile Olympias with you. I
know that she will be persuaded for her son Alexander's
sake, although you do not wish to be called his father."
He said this and left.

And he came to his mother, Olympias, and said: "Mother, 61
do not be angry about what your husband has done to you;
for your own faults are hidden to him, and I am the son of
an Egyptian father. Now go to him and entreat him to be
reconciled with you, for it is proper that the wife obey
the husband." Having said this, he raised his mother to her
feet, took her by the hand, and led her to Philip, and said:
"Turn this way; now I shall call you father, for you con-
ceded to your son, Alexander. Now I have come here;
and you have accepted my many entreaties to come to you
and to forget faults. Now embrace one another. Nothing is
shameful for you in front of me, for I am your offspring."
Speaking thus, he reconciled his parents, while all the
Macedonians marveled over him.

And people who want to get married invoke Lysius' name; 62
and they do not remember that by naming him they,
whose marriage is taking place, may be separated because
of the slaying of Lysius.[1]

CONCERNING THE SUBJUGATION OF MOTHONE
TO HIS FATHER

There was a city named Mothone that had revolted from 63
King Philip.[1] Alexander's father sent him with his armies to
make war upon them. And when he arrived at that place,
he persuaded them, with the wisdom of his words, to heed
and to submit, rather than be enslaved by the force of arms.

43

64 When he returned from the city of Mothone to his father and saw before him men in barbarian clothing, he inquired, "Who are these men?" And they said, "They are the satraps of Darius." Alexander asked, "Why have they come here?" And they replied, "They are demanding the customary tribute from your father." "From whom were they sent here?" asked Alexander; and they replied, "From the king of the Persians, Darius." Alexander continued, "Why do they demand tribute?" They answered and said, "For the lands of Darius." And Alexander said: "The gods grant mankind these things as gifts to provide them food; and he is putting the gifts of the gods under tribute; it is not right that Philip give tribute to the barbarians."

65 And since he himself wished to make the Hellenes subservient to his command,[1] he called the barbarians and said: "Go tell Darius that Alexander, the son of Philip, says this: that when my father was childless, he paid you tribute. But now that he has his son Alexander, he no longer gives you tribute. And furthermore, I shall not leave you the tribute which you have taken from him, but am coming to demand it from you and bring it back." So speaking, he dismissed the messengers. And he did not deem him who sent them worthy of a letter. And his father rejoiced upon seeing Alexander acting so boldly.

66 And when once again another Thracian city became disorderly and revolted, Philip sent Alexander with great forces to make war upon it.[1]

67 And there was a Thessalonian nobleman by the name of Pausianos, who had a large personal army and huge wealth. This man lusted for Olympias, and secretly sent men who could gain her trust so that he might persuade Olympias to leave Philip and become his wife. But Olympias did not agree to do this. And Pausianos made the following plan upon learning that Alexander was going to war and that there was a concert of performers of all kinds of artistic songs taking place and that Philip was at the concert. Pausianos, bared sword in hand, entered the theater with other

brave men, intent on killing Philip so that he might abduct
Olympias. And with his sword he struck at Philip's side,
and he struck him hard, but he did not die. There was a
huge crowd in the theater, and Pausianos rushed to the
palace with the intention of abducting Olympias.[1]

Meanwhile, on the same day, Alexander, having won the   68
war, came and entered the city and saw a big commotion.
He asked the reason for it, and they recounted what had
happened and that Pausianos was in the palace with Olympias. He had the soldiers force back the doors, and he saw
Olympias being embraced. He had Pausianos trapped and
wanted to hurl his iron lance at him, but was afraid that he
might strike his mother. And Olympias said, "Throw your
lance, my son, for Ammon sustains me." And Alexander
threw it and struck and mortally wounded[1] Pausianos. And
when he found out that there was still life in his father, he
asked, "What do you desire?" And he said, "Bring him to
me." And he took his sword and put it in his father's hand;
and he took the sword and slew Pausianos.

And Philip said: "Son, I do not grieve that I am dying, for   69
I have been avenged; and I myself slew my enemy. Truthfully, then, did Ammon say to your mother, 'You have in
your womb a male child who shall fructify you and shall
avenge his father's death.'" And saying this, Philip immediately gave up the ghost. But he had slain his enemy too.
Philip was left with his crown,[1] and Olympias took him
and buried him. And all Macedon shared in her sorrow and
mourned him.

And, after the slaying of Pausianos, when peace ruled the   70
city, Alexander climbed up on the statue of his father
Philip, and proclaimed loudly: "Sons of the Pellians and of
the Macedonians; of the Thetalians, and of the Thracians;[1]
of the Hellenes, and of the Amphiktionians; of the Lacedemonians, and of the Corinthians; and of the other Hellenic
cities: Come with me; entrust yourselves to Alexander. Let
us invade the barbarian nations and free ourselves from
servitude to the Persians, for we Hellenes are not going to

serve the Persians." Since this was his intention, he sent a written decree to the cities.

71 And all men in the flower of youth assembled together, and all came to Macedon of their own will, as if invited by a god-sent voice. And Alexander opened his father's store-rooms and gave weapons to the youths. And he summoned to battle the men who had fought with Philip. Since they were old, they said to Alexander: "We are feeble with age, and have borne arms under your father. There is no more strength left in our bodies to withstand enemy attacks. For this reason, we give you our resignation from the army."

72 Alexander answered this by saying: "Indeed, I shall make you soldiers all the more, even though you are old men. For it is in the nature of things that old age is very much more powerful than youth. For youth trusts in and vaunts the strength of the body, and many times misses what it wishes to attain, and is cruelly betrayed into danger. But an old man first of all carefully considers what he wishes to attain and, victorious through his good counsel, is freed from danger. Thus you shall soldier with us not by oppos-ing the enemy but rather by encouraging the youth to fight bravely, for encouragement benefits both parties. Now then, go, fortify and strengthen that army with your ad-vice. For in battle it is very clear that you know that the victory you bring the city is your salvation too. In the event of defeat, the attacking enemy would come upon good-for-nothing youth; while upon the triumph of the victors, recognition for glory would be given the advisers." Alexander spoke thus and persuaded even those who were greatly over age to follow him.

73 And, having collected the original forces of Philip, Alex-ander counted and found 25,000 men in the Macedonian infantry, 2,700 mounted Macedonians, and also an auxiliary of 800. And counting these together with the men he had with him, he found 74,600 altogether, including these 25,000 and an auxiliary of 8,700; and 7,600 Thracians, Plin-thians, and Scythians, with whom he filled the need for

46

scouts. And taking all the soldiers there, of which he had 71,600, including these and the soldiers which he had from his father, he went to Macedonia.[1] And he took 41,860 talents of gold and outfitted ships and galleys for war.

And having traversed Macedon and Lake Magon[1] and the upper region of Thrace, which was completely submissive to him because of his father Philip's strength, he collected choice men there and 500 silver talents. He passed on to Likauonia and offered sacrifices with the generals there. Then he went on to Sicily and subdued some people who were rebelling against him. He then went on to the land of Italy. 74

And the generals of the Romans sent their representative, Marcus Emmelius, with the crown of Capitoline Aramazd,[1] made of gold and pearls, to say to him: "We, too, following Alexander's custom, crown you with this golden crown worth 100 liters." And when he had received their favors, he promised that, with his power, he would make them great men. And he took 1,000 soldiers from them and 400 talents. And they said that they would give him even more soldiers, if they were not presently engaged in waging war with the Karchedonians.[2] 75

And from there, he crossed the sea in between and arrived in Africa. And the generals of the Africans came to meet him, and begged him to remove the rule of the Romans from the city. And he censured their fatuity and said, "Either be noble men or pay tribute to those that are." 76

And then, departing from there with a few soldiers, he left all of Libya above him and went and reached the temple of Ammon. And he ordered the army to sail to that place called the island of Pharos,[1] and to stay there. And when he had bowed before Ammon and had offered sacrifices, he recalled the words of his mother who had said that he was the son of Ammon. He stood at prayer and said, "Father, if my mother speaks the truth in saying that I am your son, give me an oracle." And Alexander saw, in a vision, Ammon locked in intercourse with Olympias. And 77 having truly experienced the power of the god, he adorned the temple with this inscription from him: "To father, the god Ammon, from his son, Alexander." And he begged to have an oracle from him as to where he might build a city in eternal memory of his name. And again in a vision he saw Ammon, who said to him: "O King, I, the taintless, perfect ram's horns say to you: If you wish to remain eternally ageless, fresh for time without end, build a note-worthy city a little above the island of Proteus[2] over which perpetually presides Plutonios, personally ruling over the endless world girt with five crested peaks."[3]

78 When Alexander had received this oracle, he beseeched the god and asked which was the island that in fact Proteus influenced and over which the god presided. And when he had asked his questions and had offered sacrifices to his paternal god Ammon, he received directions to a village of the Libyans, where he gave his armies rest. And while Alexander was walking about, a big deer hid itself in a cave. And Alexander called a bowman to him and ordered him to fire arrows at the stag. And he drew his bow and made his shot, but did not hit the stag. And Alexander said, "Fellow, you missed your mark." From this, that place was called Paratonion because of Alexander's exclamation.[1]

79 And from there, he went to Taposiris[1] and upon inquiring, learned from the local people that the shrine was the grave of Osiris. And he sacrificed to the god and hastened on his way. He came to an open plain, and saw that it was a huge and immeasurable place which had spread out and encom-passed the property of twelve villages. And these were Steramphis, Phronetetk and Edmitos, Akonis, Epyrgos, Tetrakotis, Edios, Aponis, Skambetkh, Nepheletkh, Mem-nes, Tiatkh, and Pelasos.[2] And Hrakotis was more famous than the others for it was the capital. And the twelve cities used to have twelve rivers,[3] which poured forth to the sea; and until now, the blocked-up passageways remain. The sealed-off rivers were both the little streets of the city and its broad avenues. And there remain only two which flow

48

to the sea. The river of Hrakotis, which still flows, is dedicated to the great god Sarapis. Then there is the canal
which is supplied by the avenues, and the big river called
Khouleras, which is now the Aspetia. Then there is its canal,
which is a shrine of fortune; and the big river of Kau-
ponios. And there is the big canal and the river Nephrotes
which are now out-of-the-way places, and whose shrine of
Isis Nephrotes was built before Alexandria. And the biggest
of all is the river which is called Argeos, where the column[4]
of Argeos is. Then there is the canal of Ares; the pillars
and the canals belonging to the Kanopian river, which goes
in the direction of Zephyros; and the great river of Heracles is the harbor, for it extends from the place named
Pandita to the place called the Herakleotion harbor, the
length of the city.

Then Alexander plotted the area; and its breadth extended   80
from Mendidos to the little city of Hermes. But they do
not call it Hermoupolis, but Hermapolis,[1] for whatever
went to and from Egypt headed for that place. Alexander
laid out the city as far as that point; for this reason it is
called the land of the Alexandrians. But Kleomenes, the
Naukratian, and Dimocrates, the Rhodian, gave Alexander
this advice: "Don't make such a large city for you will
never find it filled with people. And if you should fill it,
then the lands[2] will not be able to cater to their essential
food needs. Those who will be living there will war upon
one another when they are so vast and numberless. For
small-town people are prompt with advice and help; but,
being unfamiliar and unacquainted with one another, a huge
crowd of people, such as the inhabitants of so large a city,
rebel and fight amongst themselves, having become enemies
because of their endless numbers."

And Alexander was persuaded; and he ordered the archi-   81
tects to make the city of whatever size they pleased. And
they plotted the length of the city from Dracontis beyond
the grave of Taposiris[1] to Agathemon, which is near Kano-
ron; and its width extended from Mendidos to Eleurechos

and Melanthios. And he ordered the people living there to withdraw to a village about thirty miles outside of the city; and he granted them land and he called them Alexandrians.

82   Eleurechos and Melanthios were the creators[1] of the thoroughfares from which their names came and have remained. And he thought of finding other architects for the city. Among them were Kleomenes, the Naukratian, and Krateron, the Olynthian, and an old man by the name of Eroa, a Libyan by nationality. This man had a brother by the name of Hiponemos, who advised that before making an excavation for the city's foundation, Alexander make aqueducts which would flow to the sea. And the king was persuaded, and he ordered made what no other city has. And they are called Hiponoses because he who invented them was the Libyan named Hiponemos.[2]

83   And, there is no city greater than Alexandria, for all charted cities have been measured.[1] The great city in Assyria is Antioch, which is 8 stadia and 72 feet; while in Africa, Carthaginia[2] measures 21 stadia and 305 feet.

84   And when he arrived at unparalleled Alexandria, he found the rivers, the canals, and the towns built on the land there. And seeing an island on the sea, he asked, "What island is that?" And the local inhabitants said: "It is called Pharos. Proteus[1] lived on it; and the tomb of Proteus, which is worthy of worship, is in our land." And they brought him to the top of a high mountain, the one which is now called Hero's Grave, and showed him the coffin. And he offered sacrifices there to the hero Proteus. And when he saw that in the long course of time the tomb had fallen into decay, he ordered that it be immediately restored.

85   And he ordered that the circumference of the city be plotted. They took meal and outlined the area; and birds of various species picked up the meal and flew off in all directions. And Alexander, anxious about the meaning of this, hastened to summon soothsayers and told them what had happened. And they said: "This city which has been built shall feed the entire world, and the men born in it shall be

50

everywhere; like birds they shall travel through the entire world."[1]

And they began to build the city of Alexandria in the middle of the plain. First the place was given a name so as to begin from there the building of the city. And a serpent used to come to those who were busy working, and it frightened the workers and put a stop to the work. Because of the serpent's raids, Alexander came and said, "Let it be captured by the workmen wherever it is found tomorrow." And upon receiving the order, they subdued and slew the beast when it came to that place which is now called Yark.[1] And Alexander asked that a shrine be built for it there, and they buried the serpent in it. And he asked that all kinds of garlands be made in memory of the serpent's appearing. And he declared that the excavation for the foundations be made nowhere else but on that same spot, where to this day the high mountain called the Ałbiwrk'[2] appears. 86

And when he had laid the foundation for most of the city, he wrote upon it the five letters: A, B, C, D, E; A, Alexander; B, the greatest king; C, of the greatest nations; D, in the place of Aramazd; E, descended and built a unique city.[1] And there were donkeys and mules at work there. And when the shrine had been built for this divinity, he set it upon the pillar. And many serpents came out of it and slithered into the houses that were now there. For Alexander was still there on the twenty-fifth of Tubi,[2] building the city and that very shrine for the serpent. Thus, when these snakes come into the houses, the gatekeepers worship them as kindly spirits, for they are not poisonous, like wild animals, but rather, drive out poisonous beasts. And sacrifices are made to him as being of the family of serpents.[3] And they wreathed all the beasts of burden and let them rest on that day; for, by bearing burdens, they had done their share in the building of the splendid city. And the king ordered that grain be given the guards. And when they had ground the grain and made bread, this was given 87 the inhabitants as in time of great rejoicing. On account of this, to this day these customs are kept among the Alexandrians on the twenty-fifth of Tubi. They garland all beasts of burden, and offer sacrifices to the god, and render homage to the serpents who safeguard the home, and make a distribution of bread.

88 And when he had found atop five prominent peaks the land where the pillars of the sun and of Helion are (located) and also the temple of that god, he looked for the shrine of Sarapis, in compliance with the oracle given him by Ammon; and he sought the one who is the greatest god of all. For the oracle of the gods had spoken thus: "O King, I, Phoegos, the ram, say to you that if you wish to remain forever ageless, build a noteworthy city on the island of Proteus,[1] over which Plutonios presides, encompassing the boundless realm with five crested peaks." And he invoked the god who sees everything.

89 And there, opposite the shrine of the god, he set up a great altar which, from that time on they call the altar of Alexander. He offered elaborate sacrifices upon it and stood at prayer and said, "Whatever god you are, who have the divine responsibility for this land and watch over the endless earth, accept my sacrifices and be my help in war." And having said this, he placed the sacrifice upon the altar. Suddenly a great eagle swooped down, seized the entrails of the sacrifice, and flew off into the air. It circled around and released them upon a different altar. The learned examiners pointed out the place to the king. And when he got there, he immediately saw the entrails on top of the altar. It was an altar which had been built a long time ago, and seated within there was a copper image whose nature mortal man cannot relate. And, there was, with the inviolate image, a large statue of a maiden.

90 And he inquired of the inhabitants there as to which god it was. And they said that they did not know; but according to the story of their forefathers, it was said to be the shrine of Aramazd and Anahit.[1] And in it he saw the obelisks

which remain to this day in the shrine of Sarapis outside the city wall, which at that time was at the shrine of Sarapis. And divine dedicatory writings were marked on the shrine, and the city was marvelous. And Alexander asked what the obelisks were. They said, "They belong to the world conquering king, Sesonchousis." And in letters, on the shrine, there is this dedicatory inscription which was translated for the king as follows: "I, Sesonchousis, king of Egypt and conqueror of the world, built and dedicated this to Sarapis the first god revealed to this land."

And looking at the god, Alexander said, "Great Sarapis, 91 give me a sign that you are the god of this land." And Sarapis appeared most clearly to him in his sleep, and said: "Alexander, have you forgotten what happened while you stood at prayer, making sacrifices? Didn't you say: 'Whoever you are, guardian-protector of this land, who watch over the boundless earth, accept my sacrifices, and be my help in battle'? And suddenly an eagle swooped down and put the entrails on the altar. Was it not evident to you that I am the guardian and protecting god of all?"

And in his dream, he entreated the god and asked: "Will 92 this city remain true to the name Alexandria in which it was built? Or will my name be changed to that of another king? Advise me." And he saw the god, who took him by the hand and led him to a high mountain and spoke in this fashion: "Alexander, can you move this mountain to another place?" He thought about it and said, "How can I, O Lord?" And the god said to him: "And so too can your name never be changed to that of a king of other peoples. But rather, Alexandria shall flourish and overflow with bounty; and it shall help and deliver from evil the cities which existed before it."

To this, Alexander replied, "Lord, disclose this to me too; 93 how am I destined to die?" And he said:[1] "It is griefless and good and honorable that mortal man not know in advance what the time of the end of his life will be. For men do not understand that this life seems endless and in-

53

finitely varied when they are ignorant of its evils. And so it should seem good to you too not to know your destiny, dear one. But if you ask and wish to learn about your fate, I shall tell you forthwith: with my help, you, a callow young man, shall subdue all the races of barbarian nations; and then, by dying and yet not dying, you shall come to me. Then the city of Alexandria, which you are building in the middle of the land, is to be coveted by the world; a land where gods shall dwell for long days and time to come. And it shall be surpassing in good things, since it shall have been adorned with many temples and diverse shrines, and shall abound in beauty, in magnitude, and in its enormous crowds of men. And all who settle there shall stay on and forget their former fatherlands. And I shall be its protecting deity for all time to come; and forever fresh and ageless, I shall preside over it, and strengthen the land. And the city that has been built shall remain strong forever. It shall cast light upon the fire and illuminate the infernal regions. And it shall make the south wind quail when it breathes its harmful breath,[2] so that the terrible doings of the evil spirits shall be of no avail against this city. For earthquake is to grip it but a short while, and likewise, plague and famine; so, too, shall there be war, but it shall not present great danger; rather, like a dream, it shall quickly pass through the city. And many kings shall forever revere you as one who has become a god according to the customs of this land. And when you die, you shall be revered as having become a god. And they shall have a great crowd of people on the public square and all the more because of the temperate weather. And I shall be its protector and defense, so that no hardship shall remain permanently, either earthquake or deadly plague, but, shall pass through the city like a dream.[3] And many kings shall come to it, not to make war, but to make reverence to you as one who has been apotheosized and revered. And when you have died, you shall receive gifts from kings forever. For you shall dwell there both when you are dead and when not yet dead; for this city you are building is to be your grave. And I shall quickly prove to you where you were meant to be. Take two hundred and add one; then one hundred and one; and four times twenty, and ten; and take the first number and make it the last; and learn for all time what god I am."[4] And having given the oracle, the god departed from there.

And when Alexander awoke and recalled the oracle which had been delivered to him by the gods, he recognized the great Sarapis, lord of all. And he built a great altar and ordered that fitting sacrifices be brought for the gods. And he had them slaughtered and put upon the altar. And he had huge quantities of aromatic gum burnt and piles of varied incenses put upon the altar. And he ordered all men to rejoice. And he had Parmenion, the architect, make this copper statue, and build this shrine, which brought to mind Homeric verses, as that wondrous bard, Homer, said: "And the son of Zrowan[1] made a sign with his azure brows, and his marvelous godly locks moved on the king's immortal head. And Olympus, soundly shaken, trembled." In this way, Parmenion built a shrine called that of Sarapis. Now the preparation for the building of the city was as we have related. 94

And Alexander took his troops and hastened to reach Egypt. And he sent his warships to wait for him in Tripolis. He was troubled for the army's sake, for the journey was difficult. There were, waiting for Alexander outside every city, prophets who brought forward their particular gods; and they offered sacrifices, naming him a new world-conquering Sesonchousis. For, when he reached Memphis, they sat him on the throne of Hephestos and they dressed him in a robe, like an Egyptian king. 95

And Alexander saw a statue of this kind; it was made of black stone and had this writing on the base: "This king who fled shall return to Egypt, not having grown old, but rejuvenated. And he shall make your enemies, the Persians, subject to you." And he asked, "Whose statue is this?" 96

And they said: "This is the last king Nectanebos. When the Persians were coming to make war upon the Egyptians, he, through the sorcery of his magic power, saw the gods of the Egyptians in the enemy armies at the time of their entry into Egypt. And having thus learned of their betrayal, he secretly fled. And when we sought him and entreated the gods as to where the king might have fled, the one who is god in the Sarapean temple in the underworld gave this oracle: 'Your king who has fled shall return to Egypt, not old, as he was, but as a tender youth.' "

97 And when Alexander heard this, he ran and climbed up onto the statue and embraced it and said: "This is my father, and I am his son. The oracle of your god did not lie to you. But, still, I am amazed that you were really completely vanquished by the barbarian nation; for you have walls not made by human hands that could not be taken by the enemy. For there are surrounding rivers which protect your city, and winding paths so narrow and hard to pass that it is impossible for a large army to attack you. For I, even with a small force, had to struggle to reach you because of the hard going. This is rather the justice of Providence above and of God. For why did you who have fertile land and rivers obey those who did not have such dominion? For if you had also ruled well[1] with these things which you had received as gifts, the barbarians who had not been granted these things would have perished. Since they do not have resources for war and you have agricultural skill, why should you serve those who have not? And why should those who have not take from those who have?"

98 And having said this, Alexander sought the same tribute from them as they were paying Darius. And he said, "I shall not hoard it in my storeroom, but rather shall spend it on your city Alexandria, which is in Egypt, and is the capital of the whole world." And when he had thus spoken, they gladly gave him their possessions; and they directed the king with honors through Pellousion. And Alexander

took his army, and journeyed directly to Assyria. And he made the neighboring cities obedient and docile.

And having made a great levy of soldiers there, he came to Tyre.[1] The Tyrians resisted him and did not permit his passing through their city, in conformity with an ancient oracle from a certain god, which had been delivered to them in this fashion: "If a king pass through the territory of your city, the city will fall under his power." Thus they resisted so as not to allow Alexander to enter. And the Tyrians who had enclosed the entire city with a wall stood against him. And there was a great battle, and many of the Macedonians were slain. Alexander's army was defeated; and the king returned from there to Gaza. And when he had rested and restored his army from their labor, he was thinking about capturing Tyre and destroying it. And he saw in a dream someone who said to him, "Do not be your own messenger to Tyre." 99

And he sent forth messengers with a letter which bore these words: "Alexander, king of the Macedonians, son of Ammon, and son of King Philip, and himself great king of Europe, Asia, and of Libya, speaks to the Tyrians who no longer exist. When I started out toward the nation of the Assyrians, I wished to arrive there peacefully and freely. But if you Tyrians, who are truly the very first, and I do not say so politely, stand in my way, others, too, shall learn from you how powerful the Macedonians are in the face of your rebellious arrogance. And the divine oracle that has been given you is also true. For I shall pass through your city. Farewell with wise counsel; otherwise, you shall rot with calamities." 100

And when the letter had been read before the whole assembly, they ordered that the legates be tortured, saying, "Where is that Alexander of yours?" And when they said that they knew nothing, they crucified them. Meanwhile, the king was trying to find out by what road he should enter and take the Tyrians, for he was considering a reckless action. And he saw in his dreams one of the prophets 101 of Dionysos, Satyros by name, offering him a cheese. And Alexander took it, and threw it down, and trampled upon it. Upon awakening, he related this to a soothsayer who explained the vision, saying, "King, Tyre shall fall into your power and be yours because of Satyros; and you shall topple it over because you trampled on the cheese."[1] This is the explanation that the soothsayer gave.

102 And some days later, he attacked the Tyrians; and Alexander made war upon them with the help and aid of three nearby villages, which fought bravely. They opened the gates at night and slit the throats of the guards; they devastated Tyre and razed it to the ground. What they did is spoken of to this day. He figured the three villages that had helped him and fought bravely to be the size of a city, so he named it Tripolis. He made the satrap of the Phoenicians the caretaker and guardian of Tyre, and having traversed the land of Tyre, he left.

103 Then the messengers of Darius came to him, bringing him a letter, a leather thong, a ball, and a chest of gold. Alexander opened the letter and read: "I, king of kings, kinsman of the gods, who share the throne of the sun god, Mihr,[1] and rise with the sun, Darius, myself a god, give my servant Alexander these orders. I advise you to withdraw and return to your parents, who are in servitude to me, and to remain on the lap of your mother, Olympias; for at your age, one still requires training and nursing and lap-feeding. Therefore, I have sent you, with this letter, a leather thong and a ball and a chest of gold so that you might choose which you want: either the thong, which shows you that you still need discipline, or the ball, so that you might play with those of your own age, and with that childish stature of yours, not pose as a fearsome bandit and, taking on the airs of a robber chieftain, harass cities. For even if the whole world joined together, it would not be able to undo the power of the Persians. For the size of my armies is as vast as the sands that no one can count. And there is gold and silver enough to fill every field, and this whole land.

Therefore, I sent you that chest full of gold, so that if you have none, you might give those thieves of yours enough that each of them might be able to live and reach his own village. Then, should you not accept my orders to you, I shall send ruthless men to seize you, for you shall not be so lucky as not to be captured by my soldiers. And once captured, you shall not be admonished as the son of Philip, but rather you shall be crucified as a disobedient and wicked rebel and robber chief."

When Alexander read this out, the troops were terribly 104 frightened. And Alexander, learning of their fear, said: "Men of Macedon, why have you been frightened by these words, as though they were true or had the force of reality? For Darius writes these things boastingly, but he is un- like his words. Thus certain dogs who do not have the physical strength to fight bark loud and hard, as though to show by their barking their ability to act. Thus, the chieftain, Darius, not being able to do anything by his actions, pretends to be someone in his writings, just as dogs do in their barking. But even assume that the words were true; he has enlightened us and has taught us with whom we have to fight bravely and to consider it shameful that we be defeated and captured."

Having so spoken, he ordered that the letter-bearing legates 105 be bound, hands behind them, and be taken and crucified. And they were panic stricken and said: "What terrible things have we done to you, O King, that you would kill us in this fashion? We are the messengers of Darius; in brutally slaying us, why do you imitate the Tyrians,[1] who crucified your legates? Do not set this example for the whole world." The king said to them: "Blame your king, Darius, and not me. For he wrote to me not as if to a world conqueror but rather as if to a robber chief. So it is as an arrogant and mutinous man and not as a king that I put to death you who have come here." And they said: "Darius wrote you in that fashion in his ignorance; but we see here such readiness of forces, and we have heard as great and intelligent a king as the son of Ammon and King Philip. We beseech your noble spirit to grant us our lives." And Alexander replied: "Now you are terrified and afraid of being beaten to death and beg not to die; so I am setting you free. For my desire is not to slay you but rather to show the difference between the king of the Greeks and that barbarian tyrant of yours. So don't expect to suffer any harm from me; for according to custom, a king does not slay a messenger."

106 When Alexander had said this, he ordered that dinner be prepared for the letter bearers. And he sat with them and was happy to eat and drink with them. And when they had been overcome by wine, the legates wished to tell Alexander secretly how they could capture Darius by ambush, without making war against him. The king said to them: "Do not say such things to me; for if you were not returning to Darius, I would perhaps accept information from you. But since you are going to him, I do not want to hear anything from you, lest one of you denounce to Darius what was said by me. And thus, I shall be the reason for your being killed, while offering you the grace of not being killed by me." The satraps and even the letter bearers honored Alexander.

107 And then a day later, he wrote a letter to Darius and, unknown to the letter bearers, read it before the satraps and his wise friends. This was the text of the letter: "King Alexander, son of Ammon, and of his father Philip, and his mother Olympias, greets the king of kings, him who shares the throne of the sun god, Mihr, the son of the gods who rises with the sun, the great king of the Persians, Darius. It is the shame of shames that so great a king as Darius, who is bolstered by such great forces and shares the throne of the gods, fall under the humble and abject servitude of a single man, Alexander. For the names of the gods, in coming to men, do not bestow great power or wisdom on them. Rather they become all the more arrogant and insolent, for the names of the immortals are being har-

bored in corruptible bodies. And now you have this reproach from us, too: you are able to do nothing against us,
even though you are bolstered by the names of the gods
and have taken upon yourself, on earth, their heavenly
power. For I shall make war against you as against a mortal man and king; for I, too, am mortal and am mindful that
victory comes from the Providences above. And why did
you write me that you have so much gold and silver stored
away? So that we might learn of this and, out of desire for
the gold, bravely fight against you so that your possessions,
too, might be ours? For if I conquer you, I shall be a great
and famous king both among the Hellenes and the barbarians, for I have slain the great king of kings, Darius.
But if you should defeat me, you have done nothing of
valor, for you have defeated a robber chief, as you wrote
me. But I shall have defeated Darius, the king. Also you
sent me as gifts, a thong, a ball, and a chest of gold. You
gave me this present to make fun of me, but I have received
it and taken it as a good omen. I took the thong to mean
that by my valor and arms I shall thrash the barbarians and,
having given them a mighty beating, shall subjugate them
into slavery. And I took the ball, which you had designated
for me, to mean that I shall master the world and hold it in
my power—for the world is ball-shaped, a sphere. And the
chest of gold was a great omen you sent me; for in sending
it, you announced your obedience to me. For having been
defeated by me and fallen into my power, you shall humbly
pay tribute to me."

When Alexander finished reading this before his armies, 108
everyone found it pleasing and praiseworthy. And he sealed
it and gave it to the letter bearers. And he presented them
the gold that Darius had sent him. Having witnessed his
wisdom and his great shrewdness, they went away to
Darius. And Alexander made soldiers of them all, both the
Assyrians and those who had never been defeated,[1] and he
went on to Asia.

When Darius received the letter, he was startled by it, and, 109

61

in great haste, he wrote thus to the satraps near his kingdom. "King Darius sends greetings beyond the Tauros. They tell me that Alexander, Philip's boy, has come and crossed into Asia and is devastating my land. Now you try to capture him, without doing him bodily harm; for I myself shall strip him of his purple robe and torture him, and I shall thus send him back to the land of the Macedonians, his own country, to his mother, Olympias, giving him rattles and dice, with which the Macedonian children play. And I am going to send him a Persian with a whip, as a teacher of sound thinking; he will not permit him to have the thoughts of a man before he becomes one. Sink the warships which he has brought, together with their crews, into the deep. And bind in irons the men who came with him, and have them taken to live at the Red Sea. And take their horses and their beasts of burden and let them be yours; distribute and give them to your friends."

110 And the satraps of those places wrote and sent to Darius a letter which went thus: "Vštasp and Spandiatar[1] greet you, our king, Darius. We wonder how you have actually remained unaware up to this day of the great number of peoples upon us. From these very people, we have sent you nine[2] men, bound in iron bonds and ropes, whom we found brought among us; and we did not presume to question them before you. Now you will do well to come here quickly with great forces."

111 When Darius received and read this, he, in turn, wrote them thus: "Darius, king of kings, and absolute monarch, greets Vštasp and Spandiatar and those other generals under my command. Hope for nothing whatsoever from me. And if you will regain control of your lost slaves, your reputation shows that you are men able to snuff out the blazing fury of any ignoble person who has attacked and harassed you; (yet) you were not able to endure great fear.[1] Now what do you have to say? That some one of you has died fighting? What shall I think of you who bring dishonor upon my kingship by giving way to a highwayman?"

62

At this point, when Darius had inquired about Alexander and learned that he had approached and intended passing through, he moved his troops, in double file, opposite him, near the river Pindaros.[1] And he wrote and sent to Alexander a letter which went thus: "The king of kings, great god Darius, lord of nations, has this to say to Alexander. This name of Darius which even the gods honor and have determined and decreed to be the sharer of their throne is to you alone unknown. You have presumed to traverse the ocean and have not deemed it good enough that you should go stealthily about ruling the Macedonians without my permission. Instead, you have found yourself an unrulable[2] land and proclaimed yourself king. And having gathered men like yourself as partners in piracy, you attacked Hellenic cities which were inexperienced in war. And you have always ruled over these timorous peoples, whom I consider as superfluous castaways. And you have exacted tribute from them. Now do you suppose that we are as you think us to be? You shall not boast[3] of keeping the regions which you have taken, for I know that you have judged poorly. You should have first of all corrected and reformed your folly and come to me, your lord, in servitude, and not have steeped your men in hate. But up to this point, it is my duty as a god to grant men pardon. Because fate has brought me to the point of requiring a letter from Darius, I have written you to come and do obeisance to Darius. But, however, if you are now overwhelmed by arrogant pride and act in any other fashion, then I shall punish you with an unspeakable death. And your men shall bear harm worse than yours, for they did not foster sound thinking in you. I promise you upon the great Aramazd, and my father, that I shall not mention again the evil things that you have done."

And when this letter was read before Alexander,[1] he was not startled by the bombastic words. Instead he became angry and headed forward to battle. And he led his army through Arabia to the plain, and he set up his battle line opposite Darius. And when Darius' men saw that Alexander had brought the force of his army against him, they planned to defeat him with scythe-armed chariots. Thus hurrying ahead, they reached the flank side of the area and occupied it. And the chariots went and took position on the side opposite (the enemy); and when they were in order, they formed the entire battle front. And they allowed neither the cavalry nor an attack by the army to pass through them. For with great numbers of chariots coming in every direction, they would be defeated, destroyed, and dispersed.

114 Alexander crossed to the other side and set the flank of his forces[1] opposite them. For it was Alexander's lot to organize the right side. He mounted the bullheaded horse and ordered the trumpeters to assemble and to announce war with their battle trumpets, so as to arouse the gathered troops in the din of battle. And when the trumpets sounded, the army gave a great cry, and they moved out to vast and numberless battles. There was a huge commotion everywhere. And it was a great spectacle as they struck at one another for long hours in the fray of battle. At the tip of the battle-wings, they entangled with one another; and they fought very hard against one another with spears. And with both sides claiming victory here, they separated from one another.

115 Alexander's men, however, were pressing upon the men of Darius, and they caused great destruction. The men tangled together and were knocked over and slain because of the very size of the armies. They suffered much harm from one another and much from the enemies. And there was nothing else to be seen but men toppling over. For in the thick dust, it was not possible to distinguish Persians or Macedonians, general or ruler, cavalry or foot soldier. The sky was invisible; nor could one see the earth in the great blood-letting taking place. And even the sun itself grieved because of what was going on and, unable to look upon

such great bloodshed, was darkened and covered over by clouds. After great devastation, the Persian armies took to flight. And among them was Amyndas of Antioch,[1] who had fled and gone over to Darius, although he had previously been a Macedonian and had helped them. Night was falling. Darius became frightened and put aside his chariot for he was in a bad situation; because he had been easily recognizable before, he abandoned his chariot, mounted a horse and fled.

And Alexander, eager for greater heroism,[1] went after   116
Darius and pursued him wherever he was said to be. And after a pursuit of sixty stadia he reached the chariots and his mother and his wife. However, the night saved Darius himself. During this time, he procured many fresh horses and fled from relay to relay. And the Macedonians reached the Persian side and made camp. Since it was the middle of the night, they encamped for the night on top of the corpses. And when Alexander reached Darius' tent, he dismounted, entered it, and stayed there.

Although he had conquered his opponents and had attained   117
such great glory from the benevolent fates above, he did nothing arrogant. Rather, he ordered that the bravest and best of the dead be buried; and he kept Darius' mother, wife, and children with him, in honor. And so, too, did he console the other remaining captives. And the number of fallen Macedonians was great: 550 infantry; 160 cavalry; and there were many more than 160 wounded.[1] And 120,-000 of the barbarians died. And as for booty and plunder, he collected 4,000 talent measures.

Darius, meanwhile, having gotten away safely, again mus-   118
tered troops and moved upon Alexander with a force greater than the first. And he wrote a letter to the nations that were under his command to stand by with massive forces. And when a spy of Alexander learned that Darius had gathered his troops by the Euphrates River and had camped the troops of the barbarian nations there, he wrote Alexander of the above facts.

119 And Alexander wrote: "Greetings to my general, Skamandros.¹ Come close to us with the men and forces you have under you. For they say that the barbarians are not far away."

120 And Alexander himself took his forces and passed on to Achaeia. And upon arriving there, he subdued many cities, and collected an army of 80,000 men. And when he was near the Keraton¹ called Tauros, he drove his spear hard into the ground and said, "If any mighty Greek or barbarian or other king pull out this spear, it is a bad omen for him; for his city will be pulled up from its foundations."

121 And he came and reached Pieris,¹ a city of the Bebrycians, where were the shrine and statue of Orpheus, the Pierian muse; and there were animals near him. And when Alexander gazed upon it, the statue of Orpheus oozed sweat from its cheeks and from all parts of its body. When Alexander inquired as to what might be the meaning of the sweating, the soothsayer, Melanpos, told him: "By labor, Alexander, with sweat and toil, shall you belabor barbarian nations and the cities of the Hellenes, and you shall travel with wild beasts, just as Orpheus prevailed upon the Greeks by playing the lyre and singing and by pleasant words won over the barbarians of their own will and tamed wild animals." When Alexander heard his explanations, he honored Melanpos, the soothsayer.

122 And he came to Phrygia. And he entered the very city of Ilion itself and sacrificed to Hector and to Achilles and to the other heroes. And when he saw the Skamondros River across which Achilles had leaped, and that its width was not five paces, and the seven-skinned¹ shield of Eandos, and that it was not very big nor as wonderful and amazing as Homer had described, Alexander said: "Fortunate are you who happened upon a minstrel such as Homer. [For² such as you were, you passed into his work and were inscribed among the great; although in the actual facts you fell short." And a poet who had approached him said, "Alexander, better

66

than Homer, who celebrated the seven hides, shall we write of your deeds." And he replied, "I would prefer to be Thersites in Homer's story than Achilles in yours." (Up to this point, his mother, Olympias, had shared his travel and toil; after dining with her, he sent her back to Macedon with a large group of captive nobles. And he traveled straight to Darius.

And he came and passed through the city of Abdera.) 123 When the Abderians shut the gates of their city, Alexander became angry and ordered his generals to sack the city. But they sent ambassadors to him and said: "We did not shut our gates to resist your force; rather, we are afraid of the kingdom of the Persians. For if he remain in power, Darius will destroy our city. (But when you return victoriously) we shall, without hesitation, surrender to you, the great king." When Alexander heard this, he smiled and said to the ambassadors: "Are you afraid of Darius, that he might remain in power and destroy you? Go, now and open the gates, and live in peace. For I am not going to enter the city until I have won a second victory over Darius; and then (I shall not be like a guest but like a friend to you)." Having thus spoken to the ambassadors, he hurried on, and in two days reached Boeotia and Olynthos; and he destroyed the whole land of the Chaldeans. And then he came to the Euxinos River and conquered all the neighboring cities; for there was no one who dared oppose so much power. (And, having very ceremoniously sacrificed to Poseidon, he passed on to Meotis, the rocky and unpassable lands.

When the soldiers' food supply was exhausted, he ordered 124 them to slay the horses and to eat them. Although they complied with the order out of necessity, they did so noisily and bitterly, as though he had done that purposely so that they would have no hope for the future. So when they abandoned military regulations and the customary precautions, the king himself came forward publicly to them and said: "I am not at all unaware, soldiers, that the horses which I ordered slain and used for food would be more valuable than anything else for battle. But since there was a double difficulty upon us, either to eat them and live or spare them and die with or before them, I presume to say that I picked the better solution and avoided the worse. Therefore, I promise you that when the gods help us to conquer a nation, and fill up on their abundant foodstuffs, this calamity over the horses will never happen again. I could probably find other soldiers in the place of those)] lost in this famine; but now where will I be able to find Macedonians?"

125   Having reassured the troops, he journeyed straight on to other cities. He came to the Lokrians and rested there with his troops for one day. And sending on everything that he had, he went to the Akraganthinians.[1] He entered the shrine of Apollo and beseeched the oracle to prophesy to him. Apollo told him that he was not to get an answer in his oracular shrine. And the king became angry and said, "If you are unwilling to tell my fortune, I shall carry off the tripod which Croesus the king of the Elyrgians donated, just as Heracles did to get an oracle from the gods." And so saying, he seized the oracle and the tripod which King Croesus[2] had donated. And from the underworld, a voice came to Alexander in this fashion. "Heracles, Alexander, did this as a god to a god, but you are mortal; do not oppose the gods, for your actions are talked of as far away as the gods." After these words, the true oracle said, "The god himself has prophesied to you when he addressed you by the mightiest name; since from the infernal regions, he named you Heracles Alexander, I forecast to you that it is your lot to be mightiest of all men."

126   Alexander took his troops and traveled on to Thebes. And he requested from them 4,000 brave men and tribute. But the Thebans locked the gates and did not even send messengers to him. Instead they armed themselves and prepared troops to oppose Alexander. And 500 soldiers mounted the walls and shouted to Alexander, "Either fight or leave the

city." And Alexander smiled and said: "Brave Thebans, why did you shut and lock yourselves within the walls, and give orders to fight outside? For I, too, have come to fight; but I shall fight not as against cities and brave men and people skilled in the use of battle arms but rather as against country bumpkins and fools and great cowards. For behold, I shall subjugate all men by my spear. Now you have shut and locked yourselves within the walls, and send forth a united cry. Brave men should fight on a free and open field, and to shut and lock oneself in for fear of the coming battle is a woman's act."

Having said this, he ordered 1,000 horsemen to surround   127
the city and to strafe the top of the walls with arrows. And he ordered another 1,000 soldiers to dig at the foundations with axes, two-edged sabres, and deep-cutting hatchets and very long spears and to undo and destroy those stones which had been set in place and arranged by the brothers Amphion and Zethos with a lyre. And he summoned the battering rams and set them with great force to the destruction of the walls. And this task is accomplished by a machine on wheels forcibly pushed by three soldiers; and it is fired from afar at the walls, and by its bold attack easily tears apart and pulls down the walls that had been so strongly built and set up. And with yet another 1,000 bowmen, he went around everywhere killing men in order to devastate and destroy Thebes. Fire, swords, stones, spears, and lances were hurled at the city. And the advancing Macedonian hand did not tire of intoxicating the slaying sword with blood. The helpless Thebans, whose minds had been blind, were being destroyed by Alexander.[1]

There was at that time a certain Theban by the name of   128
Ismenias, a reed player knowledgeable in songs and a man wise in speech. When he saw that Thebes was being overturned and eradicated and all who resisted, murdered, he grieved bitterly over the land of his fathers. And since he was distinguished for his knowledge of the flute, he decided to set out to take up his reeds and fall to his knees at the

69

feet of the king and sing a most suppliant, piteous, and heart-rending song, so as to bring, by the reeds' entreaty and his sad songs, the king's heart to pity. And Ismenias decided to offer the great man moralizing song and sweet speech. So, stretching forth his hands, he tearfully began to recite these pitiful verses and this calamitous song.

THE RECITAL OF ISMENIAS BEFORE THE
WORLD CONQUEROR

129 "King and son of the gods, glorious and beautiful Alexander:[1] Now by my own experience, I have learned of the god-like glory of your might. And hereafter, we honor you as we do the benevolent gods. Draw back your invincible hand from your Thebans, lest unwittingly you appear to profane your family and compatriots. For Dionysos and Heracles were Thebans, and glorious ones; and they were also the first offspring of the intercourse of our common ancestors. Dionysos was born of Aramazd and fire-stricken Semele; while Heracles was begotten by Aramazd and Alcmene. They came as the helpers, peacemakers, and safe-keepers of all mankind; and they are your ancestors, conquering Alexander. You should behave like them and be beneficent. As the offspring of a god, do not spurn and destroy Thebes, the nurse of Dionysos and Heracles. Do not devastate this city built by the bullock, for disgrace for the Macedonians will ensue. Are you unaware, Alexander, that you are a Theban and not a Pellan? This whole land of the Thebans implores you by invoking your ancestral gods with the gladness and dances of Dionysos, the reed player and guardian of the grape, and with the just deeds and benefactions for mankind of Heracles. Now, behaving like your brave and good ancestors, turn from your anger to abundant good works. Have mercy ready at hand rather than murder. Do not destroy your ancestors' gods who begot you. Do not undo and ruin this city, your own land. And do not unwittingly raze from their foundations such walls as these, built by Zethos and Amphion. For by song

and the sound of the lyre are you son of Aramazd, whom his bride, the daughter of Nychteos, secretly bore when she was frenzied by dance. Cadmos built these foundations and the great towering buildings. Here he took as bride Harmonia, whom foam-born Cypros bore upon mating with the Thracian adulterer. Do not senselessly ruin your own farm lands nor set fire to all the walls of the Thebans. This is the home of King Labdakus. Here the evil spirit entered marriage; his lamentable and sorrowful mother (wed) the wretched patricide Oedipus. This was the shrine of Heracles; but before that, it was the home of Amphitryon. Here, Aramazd lamented, counting three nights as one. You see those neighboring houses ablaze, still dripping heaven's vengeance. There, Aramazd once smit the desirable Semele for whom he lusted; behold, in this fire, she bore Hraphiotian Dionysos, the grape guardian. Here Heracles went mad; and here too Heracles in madness rose and slew his wife Megara, and riddled his children with arrows. This altar, which you see built high to Anahit, has been marked out as an old altar, in which (was) Heraclit too; and in it, Heracles, while sewing a robe for Arkada, was scalded in the blood of a serpent by Philoctetes. These are the god-inspired words of the untainted, innocent one, the verses of Tiresias, who (belonged) to three nations and centuries. Here, too, is the river which Tritonia, mad for Athamas, transformed and changed to a woman. Here aiming at a pheasant, he slew his son, Learchos, with an arrow. Here, Ino[2] ran and fell into the fathomless deep with Melicertes, her child, in madness. Here blind Oedipus was driven away by the orders of Cretos, whose staff breathed war. And this is the river in the middle of Citheron which bears frenzied water from Isminos. (As for) the pine tree which you see there grown tall with branches, here, the wretched Pentheus was cut into pieces by the mother who bore him, for wanting to see the Panthean dancers. You see a spring which pours blood-colored water, behind which sounds the frightful cry of a bull. This is the river of the embraces of the wicked.[3] You see the elegant wife of Lykos, who had the tall mountain as her school. Formerly she was our Sphinx[4] to whom was attributed the character of a miracle worker while she was working discontent among the people. Oedipus in slaying her took care of many worries. This is a fountain of the gods, a marvelous spring of waters from which lovely nymphs and waters flow simultaneously. (In it) Artemis descended and having washed and bathed and dried her body, she grew resplendent. Divine Actaeon, it is not fit to tell, saw the bathings of the daughter of Leto here. His body was completely transformed, and because of the baths, he was hunted down by carnivorous dogs. And his children made war upon Thebes. To this seven-fold foaming river, Poli(ni)ces led the people of Argos, a lance-bearing force. At these walls, Cappaneus was set ablaze; and those gates are called the Electrians'. They leave through these open and inviolate doors; Amphiareos opened them and went to the Ogygian land, which is locked by three gates. He slew Hypomendota, the son of Hiposthenos, who had fallen into the hands of thieves at these gates. Parthenopos was called the murderer of ten thousand at these gates, when he came to this land. Tougeus, the Calidonian, taking heart, came and stood there. Here Coulenices and Okles fought one another. Hither Adratos fled and died. These doors and this city of the Thebans defeated the ambuscade of the Argives."

130 Thus, Ismenias, bowed at the feet of Alexander, waxed effusive, and beseeched the king.

131 At this point, the emperor became angry at the bard, Ismenias, for he was very annoyed by all the fairy tales. He fixed his eyes upon him for a long while; then, gnashing his teeth, he said angrily: "What are these fairy tales? You most evil offspring of the race of Cadmus, wild and wicked offshoot of a wretched stock, man most evil and loathsome to the gods, Ismenias, you relic of sorrow, who is blind in eye and in spirit, too. Did you mean to beguile Alexander by recounting these artful fabrications? I shall

still devastate this entire city; I shall ravage it by fire; I shall turn to ashes the roots of those ancestors. For if you know my ancestry and my origin and who my parents were, was it not your duty to preach thus to the Thebans: 'Alexander is our compatriot. Let us not make war against our fellow countryman. Let us give him the support of our armies. Let us help our co-citizen and compatriot, Alexander. It would be to our glory and would strengthen this stock if the Macedonians intermingle and collaborate with the Thebans.' But since you were able neither to refrain from seeking to revenge yourselves, nor to effect it, for your effort to fight turned into a feeble disgrace, then your entreaties and supplications are servile and senseless. For, since you were not able to choose honor as you intended, you can fight with Alexander. But this is good neither for the Thebans nor for you; for as the end appears, I shall set Thebes itself ablaze; and at the same time I shall burn to a turn Ismenias, the best of the pipers, for he helped and protected the inhabitants. Thus shall I order that the sound of the twin reeds boastfully recount its Boeotian[1] capture."

Then he ordered his soldiers to undermine and cast down 132 the seven-gated walls of the city of the Thebans; and once again Citheron gave refuge to the Thebans; and Ismenias[1] himself was dripping with the blood which flowed from his body. And the walls and the city of the Thebans were torn down. And everywhere they were grief-stricken by the slaughter; and the walls were destroyed. And there was much tear-shedding and terrible lamentation, moaning and grieving, sobbing and crying. Meanwhile, Ismenias, having properly tuned the sound of the twin reeds, stood on the roof-tops, as the Macedonian ordered, playing the flute, for the possessions of the Thebans now belonged to Dionysos. Thus all the walls of the Cadmeans fell, and the palace of Lykos and the home of Labdakos, in worship to earth's first command. He spared Pindar, and left unharmed his tomb to which he came when he was a boy and had a musical talent for lyre playing. Now having returned as an old man, he slew many soldiers in the town, and few did he still leave alive; and he wiped out the name of their race. For he said, "Let Thebes no longer have a name but rather let their city be laid waste[2] since its population is so lawless." And what ensued was determined from the origin of the Thebans. Because Amphion was singing while the walls were being constructed and brought to completion, it was his lyre that built the walls in the first place. And as the walls were destroyed, Ismenias was found to have followed suit, playing the reed. So that which was set up by the music of song was cast down and destroyed by the song of music. Thus, all the Thebans perished together with their city. And Alexander proclaimed to the few remaining: "Whoever comes upon the city of the Thebans shall be without a city." From here, Alexander departed to other cities.

133 Meanwhile, the remaining Thebans sent to Delphi to request an oracle as to whether they were indeed never again to rebuild their city. And Apollo gave them this reply, "Hermes and Alcides[1] and Polydeuces, the rampart defender,[2] shall all three, by their labor, raise and restore you, Thebes." When they had been given this answer, they waited for it to happen.

134 Meanwhile, Alexander came to Corinth and found the Isthimian games taking place there. And the Corinthians beseeched him to conduct the Isthimian games. And the king acceded to their wishes and went in and took his place. The fighting contest came on; and the victors were crowned by the king, and he gave gifts to those who participated honorably. And one of the contestants was a champion of Theban origin, by the name of Clitomachos. He entered these three contests: the wrestling, the pancratium,[1] and the boxing. And having battled his opponent in the arena with such great fighting skill that he won the praise of the emperor, he came to get the crown for the game. The king said to him: "If you win the other two

games which you have entered, I shall crown you with the three crowns and I shall grant whatever request you make." Upon hearing this, he hurried on to the contest, and fighting bravely in the other two games for which he was inscribed, he won the complete contest and the boxing match and came to Alexander and was crowned with the three crowns. And when the herald asked him, "What is your name and of what city are you a citizen, so that I might announce you?" the contestant replied, "I am called Clitomachos but I have no city." And when Alexander learned of this, he said, "Brave man, you are so glorious a fighter as to win three contests in the same arena, wrestling, the pancratium, and boxing, and to be crowned by me with the wild olive bough, and you have no city?" Clitomachos replied thus, "It existed before Alexander became king; I have lost my land and my city." And since the great king understood whence he came and what his land was and what he would surely ask, he ordered that Thebes be built once again, in honor of the three gods, Hermes, Heracles, and Lydeuces,[2] "so that they be my gifts, and not your request." And thus was the oracle of Apollo fulfilled. "Hermes and Alcides and the rampart-defender Polydeuces all three working together shall build you anew, Thebes."

The birth and deeds of Alexander of Macedon written by the wise Aristotle are finished. Now we begin his coming to Plataea, a city of the Athenians.[3]
Rising forth from Corinth with his forces, Alexander came to Plataea, the city of the Athenians, where the Athenians worship the Maiden.[1] And as he entered the shrine of the goddess, the cloth of the robes for the sacrificial services was being woven for the goddess. Alexander inquired about this, and the priestess of the goddess said: "You have approached my goddess at a good time, Alexander. You are destined to be famous and celebrated throughout cities; and you shall be radiantly glorious." When the

135

priestess had thus spoken, Alexander honored her with gold.

136 Some days later, Stasagoras, the general of the Plataeans, also entered the shrine of the Maiden. And the prophetess of the goddess said to him, "For you, Stasagoras, a fall from power has been written." And upon receiving this threat, he said to her: "You are unworthy of your function of prophet. When Alexander came here, you told him, 'It is written that you are to be famous and resplendent and eminent in all cities.' While upon my entry, you say, 'You are to fall from power.'" And she said: "Do not be resentful, General. By means of signs, the gods foretell all things to mankind, especially to those who are most powerful. When Alexander entered this place, a thread was being woven in the corners of the celebrated purple robes. I said to him, 'Alexander, it is written that you are to be famous, because of the celebrated purple color.' When you entered this place, this garment was completed, this cloth finished, and this machine dismantled. Now isn't it clear to you that your collapse from power has been written?" The general became angry and discharged her from her priesthood saying, "You related that sign for yourself and not for me; behold it is you who have been ousted." Alexander heard this and removed Stasagoras from his generalship and ordered the priestess to resume her office. And the priestess said, "Stasagoras, I related the sign for you, and the prophecy has worked out true." Stasagoras did not inform Alexander that he was going to Athens, for he had been appointed to his generalship by the Athenians; and he told them what Alexander had done to him. The Athenians rose up and rebelled against what had happened; and they all reproached the Macedonian. And when Alexander learned of this, he wrote them a letter which went thus:

137 "King Alexander speaks thus to the Athenians. After the death of my father, I had the good fortune to take over his kingdom. And after the western provinces had been quieted by letters, and I had, by persuasion, won over and taken

possession of every kingdom, I advised them all to stay in their respective places. As for my paternal friends, the Macedonians, they joyfully received me and immediately hailed my sovereignty. And protected by the number, manliness, and good will of these men, I settled the affairs of Europe. And I destroyed the evil Thebans with evil; I destroyed the city and razed it from its foundations because of its idle pride. But now that I have crossed to Asia, I am asking the Athenians to submit. I am first writing you, not verbosely as you people do there but briefly and succinctly, stating the most important points. It is not fitting for those who have fallen under a ruler, but rather befits the rulers themselves to act in this fashion and to give orders. That is to say, you should heed and obey Alexander. So now, either be noblemen yourselves or pay 1,000 talents tribute to those who are noble."

The Athenians wrote thus in answer to the royal letter: 138 "This city of the Athenians and these ten noble orators have this to say to Alexander: As long as your father was alive, we grieved greatly; and when he died, we rejoiced greatly. Philip was thrice hated by the Hellenes. It must follow that we have the same sentiments toward you. You, the bold and willful son of Philip, demand 1,000 talents tribute from the Athenians; this means you wish to have war with us. So, since you have this noble project, come, attack us forthwith."

In return, the king wrote this reply: "I, King Alexander, 139 say this to you Athenians. I have sent our Proteus[1] to cut out your tongues without ado and bring them to us; thus, he will fix your stupid orators so that they will be powerless to trick and deceive. And I shall try to devastate you and your helpmate Athens by fire, for you do not do as I have ordered you to do. Now hand over to me your leading orators so that I may consider your welfare and take pity on your city."

When they received the letter, they took it and wrote 140 beneath it, "We will not do so," and sent it off. And some days later, they gathered together and deliberated as to what they would do. Should they send the men or should they fight? And while they were deliberating, Aeschines,[1] the orator, rose to his feet and said: "Athenians, what is slower than deliberation[2] (if) you wish to send us to Alexander? We will go forth courageously, for Alexander is not Philip. Philip was born with a willful, bellicose arrogance, while Alexander has been trained amongst us in the teachings of Aristotle; and he has put out his hand and taken disciplining. Thus, he will be docile and abashed upon seeing his teachers. And when he sees his preceptors, he will conduct as is fit and proper the kingdom he has received from his father, and which he now rules. And he will modify his attitude toward us to one of friendship."

141 And as Aeschines said this, Demades, a fine orator, rose to his feet and cut Aeschines short while he was speaking and said: "How long, Aeschines, are you going to proffer us effeminate, flaccid, and fearful words, so that we might not prepare ourselves and resist him with war? What devil of fear has come into you that you speak to the Athenians in this fashion? Do you, who with so much argumentation urged the Athenians to fight against the king of the Persians, now constrain them to stay silent and not fight the Macedonian youth, a willful tyrant who has assumed the brazen audacity of his father? And why are we afraid to fight with Alexander? We who persecuted the Persians, and forced the Lacedemonians into defeat, and conquered the Corinthians, and even put the Megarians to flight, and sacked the Zakynthians, are now afraid to fight with Alexander, says Aeschines.[1] 'Alexander will be embarrassed by our great orators, and shamed by our faces!' He has insulted us in front of everyone and has dismissed the general of the Plataeans that we appointed, and has set up Hippothos, the enemy of this assembly of ours, as general. And you say that upon seeing our faces he will be embarrassed or show us favor. Rather, he will seize us and strip us, and torture us to death. Now come let us make war upon the

ignoble and faithless Alexander. Put no trust in his youth, for the thoughts of children are untrustworthy; he can fight bravely with no consideration of what's right. He enslaved and destroyed Tyre, for they were too weak to fight against him. He uprooted the Thebans who were not too weak for him but rather exhausted from many wars. He enslaved the Peloponnesians not by going himself and making war; but by famine and by plague were they condemned to ruin. And even if Xerxes filled and blockaded the sea with ships and sowed the earth with great armies, covered the sky with weapons and filled the land of the Persians with slaves, we drove him, the great Xerxes, who had daringly undertaken and successfully mastered so much, out of Peiraeus.[2] And we burned his ships and we drove his troops out of the land, since we had Cynideros and Antiphon and Cleocharos,[3] and the other nobles with them. We who conquered them, are we now then afraid to make war against Alexander, against a child? Especially since with him are his satraps and foolish aides who do not know how to temper his brazen audacity. And now are you going to send us ten orators to him? Consider whether going unarmed will do you any good; consider it and see. And I furthermore proclaim to you, Athenians, that often ten dogs have by their barking saved from the wolves many flocks of sheep huddled together in fear." When Demades had spoken to the assembly, the Athenians entreated Demosthenes to give good and helpful advice concerning the safety of the multitude. And Demosthenes stood up and, by a sign of his hand, stilled the great crowd of the assembly and spoke thus: "Fellow citizens, I do not say Athenians, for if I were a foreigner and not a citizen,[1] I would properly have said Athenians; but now I am saying fellow citizens. Our safety is a problem common to us all. We must think soundly about this: whether to fight Alexander or give in to what he says. For Aeschines presented you with mixed arguments, not urging you to fight, yet not to forgo warfare. He is an aged man and in many meetings of the assembly has pleaded its cause. But Demades is a youth and, according to the mentality of his age, gives this sort of advice. 'But,' says Demades, 'the Athenians drove Xerxes away. Cynideros was there, and Antiphon was fighting and Cleocharos was making war, and Boyidrimos was battling from ships, and again, too, Erechtheus was defending us, and Andimachos took heart and conquered.' And now, Demades, get those men and we shall make war on Alexander. We shall entrust ourselves to the strength of those you mentioned. But since they do not exist now, we are not going to fight. For each epoch has its own strength and law. We, the orators, are able with words to make great speeches among the people; but we are weak in donning arms and leaping into battle. Although Xerxes had great and powerful armies, he was defeated at that time; and the affair went the way we wanted it, because Xerxes was found weakened.[2] But Alexander has entered thirteen wars and has never been defeated; rather many captured cities have accepted him and found that this was the means to their salvation. The Tyrians were weak at the time of the war with Alexander! This was the reason the Tyrians defeated Xerxes in sea battle and set fire to his ships. The Thebans were weak! They, who have been fighting since their city was built and have never been defeated, but they were subjugated only by Alexander. Demades says that not he but rather famine defeated the Peloponnesians. Yet Alexander had sent them grain from Macedon. And when Antigonos, the general, said, 'Alexander, are you sending grain to those with whom you are preparing to fight?' He replied, 'Yes, indeed, for I shall defeat them by fighting, and they shall not be wrecked by famine.' Yet, without having been in the least harassed, you are in revolt; and you are angry that he deposed Stasagoras from his command. In the first place, Stasagoras had rebelled; for he said to the priestess, 'You said to Alexander that it was written for you to be famous throughout cities and you say that it is written for me to

80

be cast down from my command; so I shall now cast you down from your office of prophet.' Should not the king, then, upon hearing this, be justly disturbed about the doings of Stasagoras? Is a general the equal of a king? Are you angry at the Macedonian because he deposed Stasagoras from his command because the latter was an Athenian; and do not blame Stasagoras for dismissing the Athenian priestess? Yet Alexander acted to avenge us, for he deposed him from his command, while, in courtesy to us, he restored (her to) the office of prophet."

When Demosthenes had spoken thus, there was much applause from the Amphictyons[1] and there was a confused and indistinct din of voices. Demades remained still, and Aeschines gave his praises; Lysius confirmed it; Plato approved it; and Dimocrates gave his advice, Dionginos his approval, and the other Amphictyons pondered it. And the populace as a whole agreed with what Demosthenes had said.   143

And in turn Demosthenes said: "We shall continue our reply. 'Xerxes,' says Demades, 'made war.' He blockaded the seas with ships and sowed the land with troops. He obscured the sky with arms and filled Persia with Greek prisoners. And he captured and took into his power the Greeks. But of those that have opposed him, this man[1] has made not slaves but soldiers. And those who were his enemies, he made his auxiliaries. For Alexander has ruled all in this way; and he has maintained his power by doing kindnesses to his friends. And the Athenians, who are the friends and counselors of Alexander, are seeking to cease being such by speaking as enemies. It is the shame of shames for you, the preceptor and teachers of Alexander, to appear as fools. Not one of the Greek kings has entered Egypt except Alexander; and he did this not for making war but in order to ask an oracle of the gods as to where he should build a city to immortalize his name. And then he laid its foundations and built it. And since[2] it is very clear that when any task has been started rapidly, its completion, too,   144 comes quickly into view, he went on to Egypt which was under the rule of the Persians. And the Egyptians begged to join his campaign against the Persians. That wise man gave them this answer: 'It is best for you Egyptians to work at the overflow of the Nile and the cultivation of the land, rather than to arm Ares' boldness[3] and to make Egypt subservient to him. Alexander shall not be the high and mighty conqueror of the whole world, for a king is nothing unless he have fit and decent land.' Alexander, the first of the Greeks, took Egypt, thus becoming the first of the Greeks and of the Barbarians. How many myriad companies will that land feed? Both those who have settled there and those who fight in war. How many empty and unpopulated cities will she fill and populate? She is as rich in population as she is in wheat. And whatever the king requests from her, abundantly she supplies; and if he wishes troops, she gives them; if he requests grain, she has enough to give to the point of satiation; and if he wants gold for tribute, he gets it. And do you Athenians wish to make war on Alexander who has such great resources for the sustenance of his armies? Even if it were our will and desire to make war on Alexander, the times do not permit it."

145 When Demosthenes had spoken thus at the community assembly, they all unanimously approved sending Alexander the crown of victory, made of fifty litres of gold, together with their personally committed assistance and also the gratitude of the eminent Athenian messengers; but they did not send him the orators. And the messengers went and met him in Plataea and presented him the decision in favor of his taking over the kingship.

146 And when he read and learned of Aeschines' defense and Demades' recalcitrance, and the people's credulity, and the advice of the Amphictyons, he wrote them a letter that went thus: "I, King Alexander, son of Philip and of mother, Olympias, write thus to you wise orators and teachers of Athens. Since this is the will of Providence above, I am to rule until I subject all barbarians to the

Hellenes. Thus, I sent to you for ten of your orators to come to me, not that I might do them any harm, rather, that I might receive them joyously as preceptors and teachers. For I did not presume to appear amongst you in person with an army lest you think me an enemy of yours; rather (I thought I would approach you) through your orators instead of my troops so that I would keep you free from all fright and fear. But you who have been reproached in these matters bear something else in your hearts against me; it is not so much the rule over your persons as it is that I for once have decided to work with the Macedonians. For when my father was fighting with the Zakynthians, you helped and supported the Zakynthians. But when you were fighting with the Corinthians, the Macedonians helped and supported you; and they disengaged and drove the Corinthians away from you. And although you had erected the bronze statue of Athena in Macedon, you tore out and cast down the portrait of my father intended for the temple of Athena. The payments of retribution have been just; you have received from us as much as you paid. Therefore, do not be encouraged to transgress against me. You are frightened that the kingship will fall to us; and you have to avenge yourselves. It has scarcely ever been my intention to do these things to you, for I, too, was an Athenian. But when in fact have you ever thought kindly of the glorious among you? You shut up Euclides in prison, who had given you good counsel, which was useful to you against Cavos.[1] You vilified Alcibiades,[2] who served you nobly as general. Socrates, the very school of distinguished learning for Hellas, you slew. You were ungrateful to Philip who helped and supported you in three wars. Are you slandering Alexander because of General Stasagoras, who was culpable and false to me and to you, because he cast out of the shrine the priestess of the goddess, who was Athenian; while I granted her her prophet's office again? I approve the arguments your orators made among you on your behalf. Aeschines gave you advice which befitted you; and Demades spoke bravely and well in the community council; so, too, Demosthenes, who advised you to your benefit. And now once again, brave Athenians, pay heed, and have no fear of suffering evil. For this would seem unthinkable impropriety to me; for I am fighting with barbarian nations on behalf of freedom, and not to destroy Athens, its showplace."

147 And after Alexander had written to the Athenians in this fashion, he immediately took his forces and came to the land of the Lacedemonians. But they resisted him, wishing to show their courage and to shame the Athenians, who had not resisted him with war. So they shut the gates and set the troopships ablaze; for they were more skilled in naval warfare than in being brave warriors on land.

148 When Alexander heard of their story[1] favoring war, he sent them first a letter which said: "I, Alexander, king of the Macedonians, write to you Lacedemonians advising you to preserve the integrity of whatever ideals[2] you have inherited from your ancestors. But civil greetings will come later only if you are worthy of receiving my polite salutations. Now you who are brave and undefeated warriors, see to it that you are not brought down from your glory. Who knows but that perhaps, while desiring to show off your strength to the Athenians, you may be ridiculed by them by being defeated by Alexander. So come away there from your ships and voluntarily abandon the futile hopes of those plans lest that fire consume you in its flames."

149 The letter was thus read to them. The Lacedemonians did not agree, but instead set out to fight with all their might. But when those who stood armed upon the ramparts had been knocked down, and what was on the ships had been set aflame, and the remaining ships had been consumed by fire, they came in supplication to the king begging they be not enslaved.[1]

150 And heading away from there, Alexander moved on to the lands of the barbarians. And Darius assembled his generals and asked them for advice as to what should be done. And

he said: "As I see from his ascent, Alexander is fighting his way forward toward us. I used to think of him in terms of a bandit; but behold, he has undertaken and is doing kingly deeds. And as great as we Persians seem to be, Alexander appears still greater in the daring he has assumed. It seems to me that I sent him a whip and a ball with which to play with those his own age and be educated. But he has completed his education and has overtaken me, his teacher; and he is coming to conquer all. Now come, let us think about the common welfare, and from that point of view find a solution for the conduct of our affairs, lest by dismissing the valiant Macedonian as nothing, and being swollen with pride in this so great Persian kingdom, we be captured along with the whole country.[1] But now, I fear that perhaps at this time the greater be found inferior to the smaller and that Providence above is passing the succession to my crown to him. Now we must retreat and abandon Hellas so that we might rule the great barbarian nations we have captured; and let us not, in attempting to maintain hold on Hellas, destroy the Persians."[2] Thus spoke Darius.

And Oxydarkes,[1] the brother of Darius, said to this: "Look,   151 you have already started to aggrandize Alexander, and you are encouraging him all the more to attack the Persians by giving way and abandoning Greece. Be like Alexander yourself, and in that fashion you will keep your kingship strong. For he does not entrust the war to his generals nor his satraps, as you do to your satraps; rather he himself is general, satrap, and king. And not trusting to his soldiers, he himself is the first of all to leap into battle, valiantly putting aside his royal status and protecting his troops. And when he has fought and won the contest, he takes on again his crown." Darius asked, "And how shall I resemble him?"

And another general said this very thing: "Alexander has   152 won all things by never procrastinating, by bravely overcoming all problems, and, true to his nature and appear-

ance, by modeling the pattern of his behavior on the lion."
And Darius said, "Do you actually know that for a fact?"
And he replied: "When I was sent by you to Philip, his
father, to demand tribute from the Macedonians, I discov-
ered and learned of his aggressive character and the
strength of his mind and the nature of his genius. Now
summon and call the satraps of this vast land; for your
nations are many: the Persians, and Parthians, the Ilamians,
Babylonians, the Mesopotamians,[1] and the Libyans, as well
as the Indians; and I shall also list the home of Šamiram.[2]
Now your nations number 180; draft soldiers from them,
and if you can find a way, their gods, too. For although
we barbarians are not able to conquer the Greeks by bodily strength, still we may terrify the enemy by the vastness
of our mass."

153   And another[1] in turn said: "You have given your king good
counsel. But it is worthless; for a single plan of the Greek
mind will overcome and disrupt the great hordes of barbarians, just as a single Laconian dog may harass many
flocks." When they had thus taken counsel, Darius assembled the mass of warriors.

154   And Alexander passed through Cilicia. There was a body
of water called Oceanus[1] there. Its water is clean, clear,
and crystalline. The king wished to bathe in it; and he
stripped[2] and bathed in the water and came out refreshed.
But the bath did not turn out to be a factor favorable to
his health; for his head ached from catching cold, and he
suffered from intestinal pains. When Alexander was
stricken by sickness, the Macedonians were terrified in
their hearts lest Darius, upon learning of Alexander's sickness, attack with his troops. Thus Alexander's single person
was the spur and encouragement of the spirits of so many
soldiers.

155   And there was a man there named Philip, who was a beloved friend of the king, and a fine and skilled physician.
He promised to give Alexander medicinal potions and to
drive away from him the evil of the sickness. And the king

agreed to take the medicine Philip prepared. A letter was handed to Alexander, sent by General Parmenion, to the effect that Darius had persuaded Philip, the physician, to slay Alexander by drugging him, if he found a propitious moment, by promising to give him his sister, whose name was Gagipharta,[1] as a wife, and to make him co-ruler of his kingdom. And Philip had promised Darius to do this. And when Alexander read the letter, he was not at all troubled for he knew Philip's character and what tender solicitude he had for him. He put the letter under his headrest.

Then Philip, the physician, came and tendered him the cup   156
of medicine saying, "Drink, my lord and king, and you shall be freed from that sickness." And Alexander took the cup in his hand and staring steadily at Philip's face, he said, "I drink, Philip, trusting myself to you." The doctor said, "Drink, King, and have no fear, for that medicine is unreproachable." And the king replied, "Look, I am drinking." And then he drank down the medicine. Then after he had drunk it, he put the letter in the other's hands. And when he had read the accusation against him, he said, "My lord, Alexander, you shall not find me such as these words indicate."

And when Alexander was delivered from his ills, he em-   157
braced Philip and said: "What great feelings of friendship I have for you! For I had received that letter before the medicine. But only after I had drunk it, did I hand you the letter; for I entrusted myself to your honor, knowing that Philip would not look upon Alexander with malice." The physician replied: "Alexander, now put to death the one who sent you the letter, Parmenion. For it is he who urged me to kill you with drugs so that I might take to wife Darius' sister Gagipharta. And when I, my lord, was unwilling, see with what viciousness he sought to destroy me." Having verified this and found Philip, the physician, guiltless, he put Parmenion to death.

And taking his troops thence, he came to the land of the   158
Medes and hastened to enter great Armenia. And when he

had won them over, he traveled on many days through the waterless lands and snake-infested ravines. And having traversed Ariake, he came to the river Aracani,[1] which flows from the flowery hills of the Angł province to the source of the Euphrates opposite the Ararat mountain.[2] And having bridged it with arches and iron bars, he ordered the troops to cross. When he saw that they were afraid, he ordered the beasts of burden, wagons, and the food for all be crossed over first; and then he ordered the troops to cross. And when they saw the flow of the river's current, they were afraid that the bridges might suddenly come apart and collapse. Since they could not be induced to cross, the king took his aides and he himself crossed first, before all the other soldiers; and then they followed.

159 In Mesopotamia and in Babylon, the great rivers are the Dklat'[1] and the Aracani, which flow to the Nile River. For it is said that when the Nile, in annual periods, overflows and soaks Egypt, who feeds the world, then these rivers, the Dklat' and the Aracani, run dry. But when it recedes and leaves Egypt, they fill to overflowing.[2]

160 Therefore, when Alexander and the whole army had passed, he ordered that the bridge over the Aracani be demolished. And the troops became very disturbed at that and badly frightened. They said, "If, in fighting, we suffer defeat at the hands of the barbarians, what way do we have of passing to safety?" And the king, upon hearing the criticisms of the soldiers, assembled their generals and satraps and all the soldiers and said to them: "You offer me a fine hope for victory, having this (idea) of turning back when you have been defeated! Now this is the reason that I ordered you to demolish the bridges, so that you shall fight and conquer, and not turn to flight if you are by any chance routed. For the battle does not go to those who flee but to those who pursue. So I swear on the fates above, that when, after defeating the barbarians, the time comes for me to return hence to Macedon, I shall return in triumph with

88

you to Hellas. Only now be of good courage, and the clash of battle will seem like a game to you."

When Alexander had given these orders, the soldiers gave him honors and cheers. They stood bravely at their battle positions. He pitched his tent and set his camp there. And Darius' force was on the bank of the Dklat' River, and five satraps composed its rear guard. Both sides engaged in battle with one another; they fought bravely. 161

Now one of the Persians who had come and taken on Macedonian arms as if he were a Macedonian soldier and auxiliary came up behind Alexander, struck Alexander's crown, and smashed his helmet. And he was seized by the soldiers and they took him and stood him before Alexander, who said to him, "Who are you, brave man? Why did you want to do this?" And he replied: "Alexander, do not let my Macedonian arms deceive you, for I am a Persian, a satrap of Darius. I approached Darius and said, 'If I come back and bring you Alexander's head, what will you give me?' And he promised to give me a royal domain, and his daughter as wife. And I came here on my own and did not carry off the affair." Upon hearing this, Alexander called his generals to him, and while they were looking on, he set him free right in front of them, saying, "Men of Macedon, soldiers should be this single-purposed." And the defeated barbarians, lacking sufficient food, hastened on to enter the land of the Bactrians; but Sk'andar[1] stayed there since he was in control of their lands. 162

And again another of Darius' satraps risking death came to Alexander and said: "My lord King, I am a satrap of Darius, and I have accomplished great things for him in war, but had no thanks from him; for he did not render me the value of the things I did. Therefore, give me 10,000 soldiers from your armies; with them and my soldiers, I shall attack his armies and hand the king of the Persians over to you." Alexander replied: "I am grateful for that. Go and help your own king; for I would not entrust strangers to you who have betrayed your own people." 163

164 And they who were the satraps in those regions wrote to Darius in this fashion: "To you, our King Darius, Vštasp and Spandiatar greet their lord. Earlier, too, we disclosed to you Alexander's incursion upon our people; we now again notify you that he has come to this region, has seized our land, and slain very many Persians. And we stand to perish in the peril of death. So rush immediately with many troops to reach us before he does. And do not let him get near you, for the Macedonian army is most powerful and more numerous than ours. Farewell, our lord."

165 When Darius received this and read it, he sent Alexander a letter of this sort: "King Darius makes this announcement to Alexander. You have written me an arrogant letter whereby you ask us to meet you. Behold, have I not passed Ankoura[1] to bring the gods of the Orient to dwell where the sun sets? And I bear witness before the gods to the things you have brought upon me. For I shall consider my mother gone to the gods, that I do not have a wife, and that the children do not exist at all. Still, I shall not cease petitioning my enemy. For it was written to me that you were kind to my family; and if you would do a further act of righteousness and defend my interests, you would be willing also to come to me, and in that way offer godly honors to my family.[2] You have the jurisdiction hereafter not to protect my family but instead to torture them as children of the enemy. For by doing them kindness you shall not be able to make me a friend, nor by doing evil, an enemy; for I reckon both as one. Now give me your final answer, so that we might know the value of our kindness."

166 And upon reading this, Alexander smiled broadly and wrote this answer in return: "Alexander, the king of kings, greets King Darius. The gods shall censure to the very end your empty pride, your garrulousness, and your inane and futile chatter, for you never cease blaspheming and entertaining vain thoughts. Be aware, now, that I did not honor your family out of fear; and I was not tender to them in the

hope of coming to a reconciliation, so that, when I came to you, you would be grateful to us. For my crown is not of less value than yours. Nevertheless, my piety is not for everybody but for your family especially, since I call them those who have fallen from heaven to earth.[1] Now I am writing you a final letter. I have decided to act otherwise toward you than with love and friendship."

And when Alexander had answered him, he prepared for war. And he wrote an edict to the satraps under him, which went thus: "I, King Sk'andar, who am also Alexander, greet the satraps who are subject to me, those of the Phrygians, Gamrians, Cilicians, Arabs, and of the other nations. I want you to prepare tunics for big men and send them to the Assyrian city of Antioch. And send the skins of however many four-legged animals that die also to the Assyrian city of Antioch so that the soldiers may find the wherewithal to produce their needs of leg armor and shoes and weapon cases, of which each of you knows the number. Do this and forward those things to Antioch. For 3,000 camels have been readied for service from the Aracani river to Antioch. And we have also ordered that the 3,000 camels which are in Antioch be assembled, some to transport materials into town and others to take them away and thus give uninterrupted service. And they shall be ready. Farewell."

And Darius' satrap wrote him thus about the situation at hand: "To Darius, my lord, greetings from Notareses. I am afraid to write this sort of thing to you, but I am compelled to do so by the present happenings. Be informed, my lord, that Kosares has been wounded and two great nobles have died. After Kosares was wounded, he went to his tent, and the enemy took whatever was useful to them. And Annias and whatever nobles were under his command have gone on over to Alexander. They set fire to the royal domains and took with them those who were concubines there. They slew the sister of Mithridates and have put fire to the land."

169 When Darius heard this, he wrote also to the Pitaki, who were nearby satraps, to get prepared and come forth from there. And he wrote to those who were kings nearby to the effect that "We are prepared to wipe away our sweat and pit ourselves against the Macedonians. I do not intend to greet them graciously for the things they have dared to do. And I have ordered those who are in Kov[1] to move forward." He said, "I do not think that there will be an end to these doings for a long time." And he wrote King Poros a letter begging him to bring up aid and notifying him that he was surrounded and hemmed in by fighting.

170 Poros received and read his letter and wrote him in return a letter which said: "Poros, king of the Indians, greets you, Darius, king of the Persians. I was deeply saddened by reading your letter. Even if I wanted to come to you and to think about helping you, I am prevented from doing so by a chronic bodily infirmity. But now be of good cheer, for this enemy cannot stay and resist all of us. Write us what you want, for all my forces are at your service and distant nations shall heed and obey you."

171 When she learned about all this, Darius' mother sent him secretly a letter of which this is a copy. "Greetings from Rodogoune to my son, Darius. I hear that you have called people together and want to meet Alexander in battle again. Son, do not trouble the earth, for the future is not clear. Let us live in hope of better things, lest, in acting rashly,[1] you be killed. For we still have our honor and great advantages and are not, as the mother of the enemy, treated as a slave. So I hope that Alexander will come to an amicable agreement."

172 And when Darius had read the letter, he secretly wept, remembering his family, and was troubled in spirit. But he considered the land of the Bactrians his bulwark in war.[1]

173 Now Alexander had taken his army and was traveling to the land of the Persians. The walls of the city were visible in all their height to the Macedonians. Sharp-witted Alexander thought of a plan. Since there were flocks feeding

there, he set the grazing animals free. Then he cut branches from trees and tied them on the four-legged animals, and the flocks followed behind the soldiers. And as the trees were being dragged upon the ground, they unsettled the whole surface of the earth which poured skyward; and the dust rose as high as Mount Olympus.[1] Thus the Persians thought that the army was of immense size when they observed the vast magnitude of the air-borne, wind-producing tremors of the storm. For when the onlookers saw from afar the stormy darkness, they were left spiritless. And cowardlike they spread fear among themselves and were bereft of power and strength.

And when he had approached to about five days distance 174 from Persia, he drew to one side, and looked for trustworthy messengers to send to Darius to let him know when they might join battle with one another. While he was asleep, Alexander saw Ammon standing near him in the guise of Hermes, (wearing) his cloak and holding in his hand his caduceus and a staff, and he had a Macedonian cap on his head. He said to him in his dream: "My son, Alexander, I have come to advise you in your hour of need. For whomever you send to Darius as a messenger shall betray you and reveal to him all your clever plans. Risk death yourself, then, and, assuming my appearance as you see it, go to him as your own messenger. It is dangerous for a king to be his own messenger, but when a god helps him, no danger shall ensue." When King Alexander had seen this vision and had gotten this oracle from Ammon in his dream, his heart was bolstered with courage; and he rose to his feet smiling and informed the satraps of the substance of the vision. And they advised him to do what he was shown in his dream.

WHEN ALEXANDER CAME TO DARIUS AS HIS OWN 175
MESSENGER

Then the king took with him a noble satrap, whose name was Melteos, and three mighty horses. There was a long way to go, and he journeyed to the Stranga River. And this river would freeze from the snow until it was like a floor and as hard as stone. A chariot and a horse and anyone who wanted to could pass over it.

176 ABOUT THE WIDE AND FAR-EXTENDING RIVER STRANGA[1]

Then some days later, this river would suddenly melt and become a deep-flowing current, grasping in its current and dragging along anyone it might seize passing through it. But Alexander found it frozen. And assuming the form of Ammon which he had seen in his dreams, he mounted a horse[2] and crossed over alone. And Melteos begged to cross with him, "lest," he said, "there be some need of help." Alexander said to him, "Wait for me here with your two horses, for," he said, "I have as my helper him who commanded me, in the vision, to assume this appearance and to go alone." Having said this, he crossed the frozen river which had the width of one stade and was very deep.

177 And coming out on the other side, he passed on to the gates of Persia. And when the guards standing there saw him in that form, they supposed that he was a god. Nevertheless, they seized him and asked him who he was. And he replied, "Take me before the emperor; I shall tell him." And Darius was out on a hilltop. He was giving orders to his troops and organizing his forces as if in war upon the weak Macedonians. Coming upon the great splendor of Darius, he almost made reverence to him, thinking him a god come down from heaven and dressed in barbarian robes. For his body was statuesque, yet he had passed his prime; he saw that his head was covered with a crown and that the color of his robe was unlike any other. It had gold-thread decorations of Babylonian make. His shoes were Sepastanon;[1] and he had a scepter in his left hand. And the ankles of both feet were beautifully decorated alike, and they struck one another to the rhythm of his footsteps. And many strong, fully armed tribes surrounded and protected Darius

on both sides with countless men. And the guards brought Alexander before him.

And when Darius saw his appearance which he had never 178 before seen anywhere or even heard of, he asked him, "Who are you?" And he replied, "I am a messenger of King Alexander." "And what have you come to tell me?" And he replied: "I shall notify you that Alexander has arrived. Know now, King Darius, that he who defers the fighting makes very clear to his opponent that his spirit is too weak and effeminate to fight. So now do not procrastinate; rather tell me when you want us to clash in battle." And Darius became angered and said: "Perhaps you are Alexander, since you speak so boldly—not like a messenger but as though you were Alexander himself. But we must have the traditional dinner, for Alexander himself had a dinner for my letter bearers; and you shall take good care of yourself in my company."

So spoke the king, and took Alexander's hand and led him 179 into the royal palace. And the Macedonian took this as an omen concerning himself: that he was thus to bring overweaning tyrants under his power and rule over them. And he went into the palace with Darius; and when dinner was announced, he was invited in. And in the first place lay Darius on his couch; second, was Oxydarkes, the king's brother; third, Ochos, Oxydarkes' satrap; then, Audoulites, who rules Šoš;[1] and Phoartes; and after him, Mithridates. Then lay Tiridates; next, Candaules, the king of the Ethiopians; and Prince Pauliadres; and Arniphatos and Diosios were there, and so, too, Karderokedes and Alkides. And opposite them, on a single couch, lay Alexander, the Macedonian, alone. And the Persians stared at Alexander and they were amazed at the small size of his body; they did not know that the choicest clay first sent from heaven is allotted to a small vessel. And the pages constantly kept bringing goblets and serving them.

Now when they were in the midst of the banquet, Alexan- 180 der thought of this plan. As soon as he took his goblet, he tucked it into his lap. And when the servers saw him, they informed Darius. And the king rose from his couch and said, "Brave fellow, why did you put this under your robe, while you were reclining?" And since Alexander understood barbarian stupidity in its form and spirit, he said: "Great lord, when Alexander prepared dinner for his satraps and generals, he used to give them all the goblets. I thought that you were like him, and supposed Darius to be like Alexander." And all the Persians wondered with approval at the words of Alexander, for when greatness speaks, it always stirs wonder and belief in the hearer. And in the great silence, Alexander was remembered and thought of by them all.[1]

181 A certain Parasanges, a Persian prince who knew Alexander by sight because he had come before him in the Macedonian city of Pellas, when he had been sent by Darius to demand the tribute, said to himself: "Is this not he who was in Pellas; the one they called Alexander? But I must positively identify him." And he looked a second time, attentively, and said, "This is he for sure; there is no mistaking the son of Philip, for his voice has revealed him; and many men in unfamiliar disguise are recognized by their voice, no matter where they go."[1] Thus Parasanges, recognizing Alexander, leaned close to Darius, and said: "Darius, great king, and mighty despot of the Persian world, this messenger who has come to you is Alexander himself, the Macedonian, Philip's offspring, a fine man."

182 And when Alexander heard this, and perceived that the Persians recognized him, and heard the clamor and uproar being made at the royal banquet, he rather hesitated. And when he had considered the possibility of confounding them and leading them astray, he got up and ran out, carrying the golden goblet in his robe. And as he was climbing on his horse to flee from danger, he saw a man standing guard in front of the gates, holding a torch in his hand. He seized it and wrested it away from the man and slew him. He quickly jumped on his horse and left the land of

Persia. And when the Persians saw his flight, they arose in arms and tried to catch the fugitive. But Alexander pushed hard and traveled on ahead, directing his horse with the torch and showing him the way, for it was deep, dark night on Olympus.[1] And the barbarians who were in pursuit did not overtake him. For he had in his hand the guiding torch; and they stumbled about in that darkness. And he was like a bright star that rises in heaven and stands on high. Those who are below it are not in turmoil, for it saves all those there in the ravines from danger. Thus did Alexander lead all the Persians.

Now Darius was watching for portents concerning himself. He went and sat on his couch and suddenly saw a true omen. The ceiling opened and an image of Xerxes, whom Darius loved, fell through. 183

The Macedonian went on through the land of Persia and came to the Stranga River. And while he was crossing the river to the other bank, just as the horse had its forelegs on the ground, the ice melted from the heat of the sun, and the horse was carried away by the fierceness of the current. But Alexander jumped off onto dry ground and the earth received him with an embrace. The Stranga seized and carried off the horse. And when the Persians came to the same river to fight, and saw that Alexander had passed, they were not able to follow. Instead they went away from there, for this river is unfordable for all men. And Darius' men said that it was very clearly Alexander's good luck. Darius was amazed at the miraculous happening and he was saddened by doubts. And Alexander walked a short distance and found Melteos whom he had left there with the two horses and told him all that had happened. 184

Then he ordered the Hellenic companies by name to be armed and to come to him all prepared. And he went and stood in their midst as Aramazd in heaven. And when he had gathered all the Macedonian troops together, he found that they numbered 120,000. The number was small, but its intelligence was great, and more important than its num- 185 ber. And Alexander counseled the troops and encouraged the willing men to the battlefield saying: "My fellow soldiers and friends, I know that our number is small, but let no one bear in his heart a lesser courage for the fight. For anyone of you baring his fists could destroy thousands of opponents. I know that the number of Persians, with all their stupidity and foolishness, is greater than ours. But there are many thousands of flies in gardens, which, on a summer day, gather and, because of their great numbers, crowd one another; but when wasps and horseflies attack them, they drive them away in a whir of wings. In the same way, a mass of those Persian flies is nothing against a very few wasps of the Macedonian armies." When the king had thus spoken, they all praised him.

186   And they traversed many rocky roads and upon reaching the banks of the Stranga River camped there. And Darius took his horde and came to the other side of the Stranga. He found it newly frozen, and he himself crossed first to attack Alexander. And the heralds standing in their midst were haranguing and calling the brave to battle. And when all the troops had been armed and organized, Darius mounted his chariot and charged forward to attack with his chariots, menacing the enemy with the scythe-like axles of the wheels, for many satraps had mounted chariots; and others were bringing up quantities of weapons which were ingenious and served all purposes. But in front of the Macedonians rode King Alexander on his bull-headed horse. And no one could come near him.

187   And when on both sides the war trumpet sounded, they attacked one another with great commotion, and made a mighty uproar, a terrible tumult.[1] And the cries and shouts of the soldiers produced a thundering of the clouds. For, they had most eagerly assembled and come to the task of making war. Some started to throw rocks, some fired arrows up to the sky as if to cover it and darken the brightness of the light of day; others, half-massacred bodies, lay

98

on the ground, all soaked and stained in the spilled blood. And many on the Persian side perished by the sword.

And Darius turned back, twisted the reins of his chariot, 188 and fled from the crowd, away from all the fighting. And the scythes of the moving chariot mowed down the densely crowded Persians as farmers in the fields mow husks. And Darius himself and those who were with him reached the Stranga River. Finding the river frozen, they drove their chariots straight on across. But when another group of soldiers attempted to cross the river, the ice melted beneath them, and the current seized all who had not yet crossed. And those who did not manage to cross the river were mercilessly slain by the Macedonians.

And Darius fled and took refuge in his palace. He threw 189 himself upon the ground and, choked with tears, broken-heartedly lamented having lost such a great number of soldiers and having made a desert waste of the whole Persian land. And Darius, gripped by such sick doubt, lamented his fate, saying: "Woe on these inescapable, danger-laden, and disastrous uncertainties. For I, so great a king of kings, Darius, who have subdued so many nations and subjugated many cities, who shared the throne of the gods and rose with the sun, now mere fugitive from death, am a barren waste. My mother spoke the truth; no one knows for sure what is to be. For if fate takes the slightest turn, it raises the lowest man up higher than the clouds and lowers into obscurity those who are on high." And Darius lay there and bitterly languished all alone—he who had been lord of such multitudes.

He came to his senses a little later, and got up and re- 190 gained his composure, and found his reason again. After this long lament, these dolorous sighs and painful sobbings, he tried to regain his strength and control his thoughts, once he had subdued the tide of stormy sorrows. He composed a letter to Alexander, and sent off the following sorrowful entreaties to be set before him. "Darius greets you, King Alexander, my lord. First of all, you should keep quite clearly in mind that you were born a man, so that you do not swell with pride and make vainglorious plans, but rather keep the mortal order of things in mind. For Xerxes, who showed me the light, esteemed himself greater than all men and became proud and disdainful. He had a great desire to go to Hellas with an army. And although he cared a great deal for the gold and other possessions and advantages we had gotten from our forefathers, he went and lost much gold, much silver, and many altars. When you look and see these things, avoid grandiose projects; in the name of Aramazd take pity on us who have fled to you and haven fallen before you in supplication. And on behalf of the other (god), on whose account freedom exists among us Persians,[1] free my mother and wife and children. In exchange for them, I promise to show you the treasures which our fathers placed on the earth in the land of Mina, and in Šoš, and in the land of the Bactrians. And I shall pray that you may rule over the Persians and the Medes forever; and may Aramazd glorify you. Farewell."

191   And when this letter was read by Alexander, he ordered the generals who were there to hold a meeting and read the letter. One of the generals in his retinue, by the name of Parmenion, said, "Alexander, I would take the possessions and lands which they offer and give in exchange for them his mother, wife, and children." And Alexander said to this, "And here, now, Parmenion, is what I would do." And he ordered the letter bearers to tell Darius: "I am amazed," he said, "at the way Darius pleads to save his family with possessions; and all the more that he promises to give me my own lands. It is obvious that he is ignorant of this fact. For if he were to conquer me in battle, this land is his; but since he is found defeated, he should not promise me my own possessions. For if he conquered in battle, he would have to say nothing to us concerning his mother and wife and children; rather we would be addressing him about our own plight. But I would not have come

100

at all to Asia if I had not believed the land mine; for it is not right to take things from others. As to the fact that he was the ruler of the land up to now, let him consider this his gain, for he suffered nothing for holding another's land so long." He ordered the messengers to relate this to Darius; but did not write a letter.[1]

And the king gave orders to care for those of the soldiers 192 who had been wounded and to comfort their spirits and to secure for the dead fitting burial on the spot. And he stayed there the worst of the winter and made the customary sacrifices to the local gods. Then, he ordered that the palace of Xerxes, the most splendid in that land, be set afire. But soon after, he regretted it and ordered them to stop. And he saw the graves set with much gold and golden urns, which was a sight for the gods. And the grave of Cavos was nearby. There was an extraordinary ten-storied tower; and on the topmost floor [he lay in a golden basin and there was glass around him through which both his hair and his body in its entirety were visible. There, at the grave of Xerxes, were some Greeks: some with their feet severed; others, their hands; some, their noses; and others, their ears. Some of the Athenians whose feet were bound beseeched Alexander to save them. And seeing their misfortune, he wept and felt pity for them. He ordered that they be freed and be given 1,000 drachmae and that each be returned to his own land. And they took the silver and pleaded that he distribute land to them there and not send them, who had been so mutilated, back to their fatherland, to the sorrow of their families.][1] And hearing them, Alexander ordered that lands be measured and parceled out to them; and that grain be given them for sowing; and that six oxen each, and whatever else was necessary for farming, and more things yet, be given them.

But Darius was calling for yet another battle, to strike at 193 Alexander. And he wrote a letter to Poros, the king of the Indians, to come to his help, saying: "Darius, the king of kings, greets King Poros. I have written you that you

101

might commiserate with me in the destruction that has befallen my house. Since this man who has attacked us has the character of a wild animal, he is unwilling to free my mother, wife, and children, even though I promised him my fortune and many of my other possessions, that he might decently accept these things; but he has not agreed, for he has chosen to devastate my lands. Because of these acts, I intend to wage another war against him, a very great one, so as either to drive those people away or to exist no longer myself, on this earth. To this extent has he brought me to death's door. Now it is only right that you be outraged at the things I have suffered and that you seek revenge for me from the enemy, remembering the love and righteousness of our forefathers. Now assemble many nations at the Caspian gates, that unconquerable and difficult region. I shall receive those who come there, giving each able-bodied man[1] three pieces of gold per month, and five gold pieces to the horsemen; and I shall give them also grain and food. And I shall send you half of all the loot I get from the enemy. And I shall present to you also the so-called bullheaded horse, along with the royal domains and the 180 concubines in Šoš, together with the jewelry of each. Now when you get my letter, let the first thing you do be to advise the nations around you to go assemble at the place and time we appointed."

194 And Alexander learned what was being prepared from one of the men who had fled to him from Darius. And he took his troops and moved into the land of the Medes. And he heard that Darius was at Ekbatan; and he did not think that Alexander would rule in Asia, unless he destroyed Darius' reputation. He had been told that he had fled to the Caspian gates, near the land of T'ališ, in the region of Gilanos. And he hastened after him. And he learned from someone—Gistanes, the eunuch, who had fled to him and who told him everything truthfully—that Darius was close by; and he boldly and bravely pursued him.

195 And when Darius' satraps learned that Alexander was near

the area, Arivartan[1] and a man named Besos, debauched and mentally warped[2] by nature, planned to slay Darius. For Besos and Arivartan said to one another, "Let us kill Darius and get rewards from Alexander for killing his enemy." Entertaining such an evil thought, and not ashamed of it, they thought they were doing the Macedonian a great favor. And they came upon Darius with sword in hand. When he saw the wicked ones, he said: "My lords, who used to be my servants, what have I denied you or what harm have I done to you that you would slay me with savage audacity? I beg you, do not do more evil yourselves than the Macedonians. Do not attack me in a way that is more vile still than Alexander's. Permit me to lie thus upon my terrace and lament the inequity of my involvement with fate. For if Alexander comes now and finds me slain, he, as a king, will avenge the slaying of a king." And they did not accede at all to the wishes of their king, but struck at him with their swords. But he resisted them and struggled with the two powerful young men. He held Besos on the ground with his left hand, and struck his left knee into his backbone and crushed it backwards. And he warded off Arivartan with his right hand so that he could not slash him with his sword. And the blows of the regicides were oblique and to the side, and they were not able to kill him effectively. Meanwhile, the Macedonians crossed the Stranga River, which had frozen, and Alexander came and entered Darius' palace. And when the villainous scoundrels heard of the king's entry, they left Darius half-dead and fled away until such time as they might learn what the king said about them.

And when he came into the palace, Alexander found Darius still half-alive, stricken down to the ground by the sword, and terribly stained by his very dark blood. He cried and made fitting lamentations of sorrow over him; and with tears streaming as from fountains from his eyes, he beat his breast in sorrow. And he covered Darius' body with his own cloak, and being a king himself, he grievously

196

103

lamented a king's misfortunes. Compassionately placing his hand upon Darius' chest, he spoke thus to him. "Arise from your own ground, king of the Persians, great Darius, and once again be master of your realm; rule your royal multitudes; take upon yourself your great glory, the royal crown. I swear to you, Darius, by Providence above and all the gods, that I say this to you truly and without false guile; for I want your crown to be yours alone, and so, too, the imperial scepter you held. For I sat with you and shared your banquet table when I came to you as Alexander's messenger. Now, brave one, arise and take command of your land; stand up and be brave; it does not befit a king who has met misfortune to grieve in his heart. For man knows nothing about death, and no one can boast of escaping it. But tell me, my lord king, who were the men who struck you. Point them out to me, that I might give you rest from your sorrows."

197 And when Alexander said this, Darius groaned, sighed deeply, and stretched forth his hand and drew Alexander to him. He embraced him and said: "Alexander, never swell with pride, arching your head in kingly glory; for when you accomplish a godlike deed and seem to be touching heaven with your hands, call to mind and consider the future. For fortune knows neither king nor prince, neither the peasant nor the populace. It goes everywhere, unpredictably, and does its work. See now, what a king I was, and what a wretched man I have become. I, who was the master of the earth, am dying without being master even of myself. Bury me, my son, with your glorious hands. Let the Macedonians surround me and not the Persians; let not the barbarians be Darius' next of kin.[1] See now and be prepared to protect yourself from your own people, lest you suffer harm from the Macedonians as I do now from the Persians. Also I beg to entrust to you as your own parent my wretched mother, Queen Rodogoune, and care for my wife as a blood relative. And I give you my daughter Roxiane for a wife, for if my memory still survives even in

death, two children shall be boasted of by their parents; you by your father, Philip, and my daughter, Roxiane, by Darius. Honor my sister, Gagipharta, and consider her your own sister and respect my brother, Oxydarkes, as a true king, so that the Macedonians do not trample on him. And take care of the other children as befits your sagacity and genius." And when Darius had spoken these last words, he expired in the arms of the world conqueror, Alexander.

AS TO WHERE ALEXANDER BURIED DARIUS.　　　　198

Meanwhile, Alexander commiserated in his sad lot and was moved to pity; and he wept bitterly. He ordered his body put in a casket[1] and he buried him as was proper that a king be buried according to Persian custom. He ordered the noblest of the Macedonians and Persians, in panoply, to go first; and he, the king himself, lifted upon his shoulder and alone bore through the midst of the satraps the body of Darius. And the people following along were moved not so much at seeing Darius as that Alexander was carrying him. And he set him in the grave of the Persian kings; and then, sacrificing many oxen and sheep, he carried out the funeral ceremonies. And he himself sat in power and might upon the royal throne and decreed laws and orders to the Persian land by the following edict.

"I, King Alexander, son of the divine king, Ammon, and   199
mother Olympias, write to all you inhabitants of the land of Persia: to the Aryans and the non-Aryans,[1] to the country folk and the city dwellers. For," he said, "it was not my wish to have so many thousands perish terribly, but some god or fate granted me victory over the Persians. I am very grateful to Providence above and also to the gods everywhere. You should be aware that you are to be appointed satraps whom you must heed and obey as (you did), at the time of Darius, all the generals appointed by him. You must not acknowledge any king other than the young and wise Alexander alone. And each of you should abide by the religions and customs, the laws and conventions, the feast

days and festivities, the banquet celebrations and cattle sacrifices as you did in the days of Darius. Let each man stay Persian in his way of life, and let him live within his city. And the disobedient shall be punished with death. And I make no claim to your possessions; each shall govern his own—except for gold and silver. For every man, both good and bad, will be seen taking pride in and boasting of these. So I order that all the gold and silver be used by those who live in our towns and cities. And let the money which everyone has be given as a gift to each man to use as he pleases. And take all offensive weapons and shields to the prepared and designated arsenals; and the satraps shall use this force along with their own to arm themselves. And let the customary celebration be enacted with the agreement of the satraps and generals. Let no tribe mingle with another, nor one region with another, except for purposes of business alone, and then, unarmed and in groups of twenty men. Otherwise, he shall be put to death as an enemy rebel by Persian law. And acting according to these things, all businessmen shall do as they did, and you shall carry on as in the time of Darius. And from the villages and from all you others who used to pay him a tribute of three parts, I shall take two. For I wish to make the land one of widespread prosperity and to make the Persian roads peaceful and quiet commercial arteries, so that people from Hellas may easily go to whichever Persian city they wish. Therefore, I have ordered each of the satraps to open a road from the gorges of the Euphrates River; and from the beginning of the road, at intervals of a half mile and a mile, to write upon it where the road leads. And let there be a sign if two or more roads meet, indicating whether the roads are wide (or) insufficiently dry; and let this be clear. Now, as for what was fixed as customary toll and was a problem on the roads in Darius' times, I grant this to the temples of the gods, and especially Drosabares, because I wish that they fittingly celebrate my birthday in conjunction with that of Cavos. I have ordered the satrap

106

Moschylos to celebrate joyfully my and Cavos' birthday with a great celebration; and for my festival, let both spectators and athletes be Persian; and let them be held in Persia. And I also wish that the virgin who has crowned our city, as long as she remains a pure virgin, be my mother's priestess, receiving in annual tribute a payment equal in value to her twin crown. But if nature should overcome her and make her a woman, let her be given the amount in place of a dowry. And these same regulations shall remain for the one assuming the priesthood. And the gymnastic festival shall take place in a famous, beautiful place, as in a Hellenic city. I shall make that choice myself while I am alive. But after my death, I think that the people whom I entrusted will also be able to do what is necessary. And for the war chariots, let there be awarded a golden bowl which shall weigh 1,200 staters; and for the others, a silver one, apiece, which should hold enough for a very sober man to get drunk on. And for the war horse (contest), a bowl of equal weight and a Medean robe; and he who has succeeded and won shall be present daily at Alexander's dinner table. According to the Persian custom, let him have the sacred double crown of gold, and the plain Persian robe and the golden belt and two cups worth 170 staters. And as the sign of victory, let all my satraps eat at the Alexandrian shrine, which is the shrine of all rulers of Persian citizenship who are not opposed to the king. And the regional leaders and chiefs of these contests shall be our Alexandrians. And the priest of the Alexandrian temple shall be Moschylos, who built the Alexandrian shrine, and he shall wear a golden crown and purple robe, especially on my special days. Apart from what I have ordered, let no one presume to enter the shrine, and according to all customs, let the Medes not be permitted to enter. And I wish that no one of you be your own judge when you have an affair with your neighbor, nor with anyone whomsoever, especially when it concerns important matters. If anyone be found outside of his council assembling either satraps or any other group, he shall be short-lived, condemned, and slain as an enemy of the Persian people."[2]

200 And when all this was finished, Alexander turned to his own affairs and said: "Mutinous Medes have cast down my great and mighty Darius. And I did not slay him, but others did; others, whom I do not know. To these satraps I owe huge gifts. I shall grant them the gifts they desire, and vast terrains besides, for they killed my enemy."

201 When Alexander had so spoken, the Persian multitude was troubled that the world conqueror was preparing to destroy the Persians. And seeing the sadness of the crowds, he said: "What do you suppose, men of Persia, that I am going to leave you who have killed King Darius in shame and dishonor? For if Darius were alive, he would once again be collecting soldiers for war against me. But now that he has been slain, all warfare has been stilled and stopped. So if it was a Macedonian who killed him, let him come to me openly, and take as the rewards of his bravery whatever he needs and desires. And if it is one of the Persians, let him not at all be troubled. For I swear upon the gods and on the life of my mother, Olympias, that I shall make him notable and conspicuous to all men." When the king had taken this oath, the whole crowd, in common, wept.

202 THE SLAYING OF BESOS AND ARIVARTAN.

And Besos and Arivartan, the evil ones who had slain Darius, expecting to receive great rewards from Alexander because of his pledges, approached him and said: "O King, may you live forever, Lord Alexander. We are the ones who slew Darius, your enemy." And when Alexander heard this, he ordered that they be seized and crucified upon the tomb of Darius. And they cried and pleaded and said: "Alexander, you swore upon the gods and Olympias' life that you would make the murderers of Darius conspicuous and notable. Why now, ignoring the promises that you made, do you order that we be crucified?" The king said to them: "I do not act on your entreaties, but on be-half of my people. Persians, it was possible by no other means to find them so easily and to make them come forward but by slandering Darius' death for a little while. For it was thus my purpose to sentence his slayers to great mortal punishment. For those who slay their own king would be all the readier to have the brazen audacity to attack even me. And evil ones, you were not made a false pledge; for I swore to make you conspicuous and notable to all men. Now you shall be conspicuous and notable hanging on that cross." When Alexander had so spoken, everyone praised him. And those evil men were crucified at Darius' grave.

And a few days later, when Sk'andar had restored peace to the city, he said to the populace, "Whom do you wish to be the satrap of this city?" And they replied, "We implore your goodness, our sovereign lord, to grant us Adou-lites,[1] Darius' uncle." And Alexander granted it. 203

And he wrote Darius' mother and wife a letter which said: 204
"King Alexander greets Statira and Rodogoune. As god has wished, we have defeated Darius who opposed us. I prayer-fully sought and hoped to take him alive under my royal staff. And I wanted so much to heed his wishes. But Darius was captured after he had been wounded by his own men. And while he was breathing his last, I pitied him and la-mented over him, sorrowing over his mortal person. And I covered him with my cloak and inquired about his mur-der. And he recommended you to my trust and gave his daughter, Roxiane, to be my wife, but he did not have the time to talk to me about the other things he wanted. Now I have pursued those that caused his death and have de-stroyed them. Having taken a fit and proper vengeance, I have banished them with bitter death from among the living. But it seemed right to me that you should enshroud his very splendid body and mourn it with your traditional laments. And I think you should hear this story, but not be filled with sadness. I have ordered that he be put in a

heroic tomb among his heroic ancestors; and I have sent his wonderful body to be prepared for burial. Now put an end to your grieving and your touching tears, for I shall set you up in your own lands to rule over whatever peoples you wish. But since some people have had the madness to revolt, stay for the present where you are until I set matters here in order, and until it is time to give the hand which he deemed worthy of my extending to Roxiane. For he truly considered it fit that his daughter share my throne. And I am very desirous that you will agree with me for I want to render her homage as the wife of Alexander. Farewell."

205 And they wrote a letter to Alexander thus: "To you, the world-conquering king: Rodogoune and Statira send you, Alexander, king of kings, lordly greetings. We prayerfully entreated the heavenly gods, who vanquished Darius' reputation and that of the Persians, to set up for you eternal glory on earth. For in wisdom and talent, intelligence and strength, you were given a nature equal to that of the Olympian gods. We know that under your care we will be well off; and in the name of fortune, we extend to you in our prayers this fine and wonderful wish: that you possess the best things of the whole world for time without end. For you approached us, who had fallen under the staff of your rule, not as slaves, but you treat us instead as people who have come from very great station. And we are no longer slaves, but rather we know that Alexander has become Darius and we make reverence to Alexander who has not put us to shame. Now we wrote to the Persians, to the remnant of that race, a letter which asked them to enthrone you as a god with Aramazd, to be reverenced along with him. And when Aramazd takes Roxiane in marriage, we shall revere her, whom you considered and chose to make the partner of your throne, as Anahit.[1] (And, for your information, we wrote to the Persian people that we now recognize Darius and that the royal scepter of Darius has been set aright and stands erect; for the great Aramazd-Alexander takes Roxiane in marriage.[2]) 'Now you should

110

bring forth all the traditional Persian gods and present them to Alexander with blessings and praise for he has raised even higher the glory of the Persians.' And at the wedding, we Persians shall announce and proclaim our reverence to Alexander."

And when Alexander received the letter, he said: "I re- 206 nounce the honor of being equal to the gods. For I am a mortal man and must fear this sort of thing, for it presents danger to the soul. But I laud and thank you and acknowledge your thoughtfulness. And I shall try to be worthy of your forefathers by taking care of you. Farewell."

And he also wrote a letter to his mother, Olympias, and 207 acknowledged the wedding, and sent it to Macedon.

And afterwards, he wrote Roxiane in this fashion: "King 208 Alexander greets his sister, Roxiane. I wrote to my mother, Olympias, about the various things that have happened to us. I asked for the woman's jewelry and clothing of Rodogoune, Darius' mother, and his wife, Statira, which I sent Karanon,[1] the Macedonian, to bring to you; for Rodogoune and not Statira is to have this jewelry to ornament her body. And now you should mindfully revere all-seeing Emeses Eutikes[2] and cast away from yourselves all strong and lasting resentment. And when you look into the present matters, you should consider acting likewise about them, since these things are right before God and man. Do not spurn fortune, but try to think respectfully of Alexander and to honor the awe-inspiring qualities of Olympias. Acting in this fashion, you shall bring great and good glory to yourself and to me. Farewell in love."[3]

Meanwhile, Olympias prepared the royal vestment, which 209 was splendid and more wonderful than any king had seen, and sent it from Macedon. And the wedding was quickly performed. And after the great rejoicing in Roxiane's and Alexander's palace, he wrote his mother, Olympias, a letter. "Sk'andar, king of kings, greets his dear mother, Olympias, and the learned Aristotle, his venerable guide and great teacher. I deemed it essential to write you concerning the conflict beyond the Tauros between me, my troops, and my Macedonians and Darius. When I heard that he was moving with many kings and satraps toward the gulf of Isos, I collected a lot of goats and tied torches on their horns and attacked them by night. And when they saw us, they turned to flight thinking that the body of troops was vast and that it was moving upon them. And thus we achieved the glory of victory against them. And on the spot, I built a city named Aycs,[1] and on the gulf of Isos, I built a city named Alexandria Kattison.[2] And from there, I pursued Darius to the approaches of the land of Armenia where the Dklat' is and the source of the Euphrates. There Darius fell into the hands of his generals and was slain by Besos and Arivartan, Medean generals. I was deeply grieved; for although I had conquered him, I was able neither to slay him nor to hold him under my royal scepter. But when I reached him, I found him still breathing. And taking off my anamesidon[3] cloak, I threw it over him. Then he saw the precariousness of fate in the present situation. And after I had shrouded Darius and honored him, I ordered those who were guarding his tomb to cut off his nose and ears according to Persian custom. Then we went away from there and came to a dense cedar grove. I ordered that my insignia be put there and the names of those who had been conquered, of Besos and of Arivartan and so, too, the kingdom of Mazkos[4] and the Medes and the Armenians and the Nomads and the whole Persian world which Darius, the great, ruled. And taking many guides there, I wished to go to the other side of the Medean desert, guided by the movement of Arcturus. The inhabitants of that place said that there are wild men and evil beasts there. Since I wanted all the more to see the places and the people, I ordered that we go see those places with a large army of natives and of our own soldiers. And then we came to a place where there was a roadway and a very deep valley. We went through there and saw deserted places and various kinds of wild animals. And coming to a place about nine o'clock, we found a forest of trees called Kanaphniton,[5] which bore fruit similar to an apple. And in that forest, there were men who were called Plantings.[6] And they were each twenty-four cubits tall; and they had long necks, and their hands and fingers were like saws. They came and gathered about us. But I was deeply saddened by looking at such beasts. I thought of capturing some of them, but when we attacked them with shouting and the sound of horns, they turned and fled when they saw us. And we slew 432 of them, and they, 164 of our soldiers. And we moved on and subsisted on the fruit of the trees, as other men did too. This was the only food we had. Then, departing from there, we came to a verdant place where there were giantlike wild men, as big as the first, barrel-chested, hairy, and reddish colored. And they had faces like lions. And others called Oxoli[7] had hair four cubits long, and they were as wide as a spear. These very powerful men came to us in tunics of rawhide, ready to fight without spears or arrows. They slew many of our group. And since many of our friends and youths were lost, I ordered that a blaze be started in order to fight them with fire. Thus the men went away. And of our soldiers, losses numbered 120,000;[8] I ordered that pyres be lit and their remaining bones be taken to Spetriada.[9] But they disappeared completely. And we quickly entered their caves and found tied to their doors wild beasts as large as the dogs we call dantakes,[10] four cubits long, three-eyed, and of motley coloring. And we saw a flea, like tortoises in our country, an earthen-colored and troublesome breed. And departing from there, we came to a place where a delicious and abundant spring rose. And I ordered the army to camp and, mindful of the carnivores, to make a ditch and a barricade around us so that the troops might rest and recuperate a bit. Then there appeared to us, about nine or ten o'clock, a man as hairy as a goat. And once again, I was startled and disturbed to see such beasts. I thought of capturing the man, for he was ferociously and

brazenly barking at us. And I ordered a woman to un-
dress and go to him on the chance that he might be vanquished by lust. But he took the woman and went far away
where, in fact, he ate her. And he roared and made strange
noises with his thick tongue at all our men who had run
forth to reach her and to set her free. And when his other
comrades heard him, countless myriads of them attacked
us from the brushes. There were 40,000 of us. So I ordered that the brushes be set afire; and when they saw the
fire, they turned and fled. And we pursued them and tied
up 400,000 of them, but they died since they refused to eat.
And they did not have human reason, but, rather, barked
wildly like dogs. And from here, we moved on to a river
that flowed abundantly. Then I ordered the army to camp
and arm themselves according to military custom and to
eat dinner in this fashion. And at that river, there were
some marvelous trees. They appeared at sunrise and grew
until six o'clock. And from six on, they shrank and with-
ered until nothing of them was visible at all. Their sap was
like Persian incense and had a very sweet and lovely smell.
And I ordered them to hew the trees and to collect the
sap with a sponge. And suddenly those men of mine were
tortured by invisible evil spirits. We heard the murmurs
of the torturers and we saw the blows that fell on their
backs, but the torturers themselves were not visible. Instead, a voice came forth saying: 'Neither collect nor hew.
Otherwise, he who does so will meet a horrible death.'
Then I ordered them not to collect nor to hew. And there
were black stones in that river, and everyone who approached these stones took upon their bodies the same color
as the stone. And there were many snakes in the water
there and many kinds of fish which were cooked not by fire
but rather by cold spring water. For one of the soldiers
washed one in cold water, put it in a pan and left it, and
then he found the fish cooked in the pan. And an hour after
he had tried this, he showed it to the others. And in the
river there, there were fowl similar to those in our land.

But if anyone approached them, fire came out of them. And I ordered that no one approach them. And we quickly moved out of there and went and journeyed about. And the guides said: 'King, we do not know where we are going. Let us turn back so that we do not once again cross difficult terrains.' But I was not willing. And many five-footed beasts ran up to meet us. They were five-eyed ones, and others were six-eyed and six-footed. And they were thirty cubits long; and they rushed upon us. And there were many other kinds: there were those which turned and fled, and those which attacked us. And we came to a sandy place where forty-two beasts emerged. They had six eyes of which only two had sight, and they could not see with the others. Moving on, we came to a place where there were headless men. They had no heads at all, but had their eyes and their mouths on their chests, and they talked with their tongues like men. They were hairy and dressed in skins, a fish-eating sea people. And they gathered there, on land and from the sea, hydna,[11] which we have at home. They got twenty-five liters worth and gave them to us. And we saw many huge sea lions slithering on the ground. And we saw, too, lobsters as big as ships. Friends frequently beseeched me to turn back, but I was unwilling, for I wished to see the end of that land. Then moving on, we traveled through a desert toward the seacoast. And not again after that did we see anything, neither bird nor beast, other than sky and earth. And we did not see the sun again; but went on through darkness for ten days. And when we came to the coast, we boarded our boats after putting all the troops and tents aboard. And we sailed to an island in the sea which was not far from shore, on which we heard human speech in Greek; but we did not see who was speaking. And the soldiers risked death to swim[12] from the ship over to the island. And a lobster rose and knocked 54 soldiers into the water. And we were frightened and moved on from that area. And in two days, we came to a place where the sun does not rise. And when I wished to instruct and send servants to see where the lands of the Blessed were, Callisthenes, my friend, advised me to approach with 40 friends, and 100 youths, and 1,200 soldiers. And later, on the way, we heard a female ass giving birth to a little one, which we joined to the army. And when we advanced fifteen miles, two birds with human faces met us, and they were larger than our birds at home. And they were crying from above in Greek: 'Why do you tread the earth looking for the home of the gods? For, you are not able to set foot in the Blessed Islands of the skies. Why do you struggle to rise to heaven, which is not within your power?' And fear and trembling seized me, since I was of course frightened when I heard the divine utterance spoken by the two birds. And another bird spoke in Greek and said: 'The East summons you. And you shall conquer Poros, king of the Indians.' And having said this, the bird flew off. And turning back from that place, we set our guiding star by Arcturus and thus came out in twenty-two days. And I put the gates together and carefully sealed up the place. And I wrote on a stone all that we had seen. And only then did I rise and go offer sacrifices to the local deities."

210   Then Alexander[1] took his army and went straight to India, upon learning that Poros was coming to aid Darius in battle. When Alexander had inquired and ascertained that Poros was coming to the battle with elephants and other wild animals, he ordered that the bronze statues that had been made in Persia be put on chariots and taken along in his train behind him. And in this fashion, he moved on through many deserts and waterless places, deep valleys, and plains. He suffered along with all the troops until his greatest princes said to him: "We have had quite enough in fighting the Persians and in conquering Darius, who sought tribute from the Greeks. Now why are we suffering the hardship of going across unpassable and beast-infested places to the land of the Indians who have done nothing to Hellas? But if Alexander in his great wisdom is a brave

116

warrior and wants to subdue barbarian peoples, let him go alone and fight; why should we follow him? It suffices that he caused many men to be devoured by savage beasts in wild and desolate places. Let him not take with him as his helpers and his fellow warriors us who have struggled and suffered in so many wars."

When the king heard this, he called them together. And he placed the Persian army by itself and put the Macedonians with the other Greeks and said: "Macedonian and other Greek comrades in arms and fellow soldiers, these Persians used to be both your enemies and mine. You have bid me to go fight alone against the barbarians, for I heard some saying: 'If Alexander wishes to fight with the barbarians, let him go by himself, alone. Let him not take us in his train.' Now I am going to remind you of this: Do you concede that I won those wars alone and that I shall, by myself, succeed in all the things that I propose to do yet to the barbarians? For the strength of my will and my counsel encouraged you all to battle, for you were dispirited and helpless. Was I not your protector in battle, at the head of the army, in face of Darius' hordes? Did I not go before Darius as my own messenger? Did I not expose myself to the danger of death? So what is the matter now? Go on back to Macedonia and save your own hides. Now do not hesitate and argue with one another. For the fact is that an army is able to do nothing without the wisdom of a king." When the world conqueror had thus spoken, they entreated him to cease being angry and to accept them as his battle companions and helpmates until the end.

And a few days later, they came to the borders of India. Letter bearers sent from Poros met him there and handed him this letter. And he read the following: "I, Poros, king of the Indians, order you, Alexander the Macedonian, who are devastating all cities, to depart. Since you are a man, what power do you have against the gods? And why do you joyously trample upon the misfortunes of others? Because you have fought with weak men, do you suppose that you are mightier than others? I am invincible. For I am king not only of men, but of the gods, too. For when Dionysos, whom you consider a god, came here, I drove him away with my power. So now I not only advise but order you to immediately leave and go to Hellas. For the battle against Darius will not frighten me, nor the subjugation of however many other nations whom, because of their weakness, luck made yours. But you think you are all powerful, when in fact you are weak. So get up and move on and go to Hellas. For if the Indians needed Hellas, long ago, before King Xerxes, they would have cast it under servitude. Now since they consider them worthless people in whose land there exists nothing worthy of royal notice, they have not turned their attention to them. For every man desires to have what is good and not what is inferior. Thus we have abandoned Hellas as worthless and we enjoy a fertile land. So now pick up and return to Hellas. Do not covet those whom you cannot rule."

213 When Alexander read this, he said to his soldiers: "Fellow soldiers, do not let this letter from Poros, which was just read, upset you again. Remember the one Darius wrote. For the foolishness of the barbarians is really uniform. Just as the wild animals, tigers, leopards, and lions and elephants in their lands, boasting of being brave because their bodies are different, are easily hunted down by human intelligence, so, too, the rulers of barbarian nations who vaunt the greatness of their armies are easily captured by the astuteness of the Hellenes."

214 When Alexander had thus appeared openly and had piqued the army to courage, he wrote this letter in reply to Poros: "King Alexander of Macedon greets Poros, the king of the Indians. Know now that you have made us all the more eager to battle you with fury by saying that Hellas has nothing worthy of royal notice, while you Indians have all bounties, both lands and cities. And you know that everyone desires to possess what is good and not what is inferior. Now since we Hellenes do not have these things, but

118

rather you barbarians have and hold them, we Hellenes covet what is good and desire to get this from you. And about yourself, you wrote me that you are the king of gods and of men, and that you are able to consider yourself greater even than the gods. But I shall attack you in battle as a boastful barbarian and not as if I were fighting with the gods. For the whole world together cannot withstand a single god's taking up arms, nor the flash of lightning or the burst of thunder. Now as the nations I have attacked in war do not awe or frighten you, so your boastful words do not terrify me." Thus was the letter written and returned.

And when Poros read what he had written him, he was 215 greatly angered; and he collected his horde of men and the many elephants and beasts that went into battle with the Indians. And when the Macedonians and Persians drew near and Alexander saw the vastness of the battle preparations, he was afraid not of the great number of men but of the beasts. For they saw the new and marvelous doings of the beasts; and they were accustomed to fighting with men and not with animals.[1] Then Alexander himself entered Poros' city in the guise of a soldier, as a messenger sent to buy food. And when they saw him, they took him before Poros. The king said to him, "Why have you come here?" He replied, "We are soldiers sent by Alexander." He said to them, "How is Alexander?" "He is alive," they replied, "and well." "Why does he wish to fight the great force of Poros?" he asked. "But I shall take care of him when he gets here." And he deliberated for a long while and personally oversaw the readying of the horde of animals. And after he had taken counsel within himself, he went to his troops.

Then what did keen-witted Alexander do in the face of 216 this? He ordered that all the bronze statues of men that he possessed be intensely heated until the bronze was like fire; and he had them taken up front opposite the beasts. And when the animals attacked them and laid hold of the

119

bronze of the statues, which looked like men, their mouths were burnt and broken. Never again did they approach anyone. With such ingenuity, astute Alexander put a stop to the attack of the animals.

217 And the Persians greatly harassed the Indians and drove them off by the shooting of arrows and cavalry attacks. And it was a great fight both for the slayers and those who were slain. Alexander's bullheaded horse fell to the ground, stricken by Poros' iron lance. And when this occurred, the Macedonian was dumbfounded, and unmindful of all else, he dragged the horse out of the battle himself, so that it would not be carried off by the enemies. And Alexander's army struggled and fought for seven days.

218 And certain of the men were very fearful and wanted to surrender. And when Alexander learned that they were preparing to surrender, he remained silent, but had his heralds say to Poros: "Poros, it is of no value to a king that so many troops be lost futilely. But merit would lie, rather, in their physical well-being, if each of our soldiers rested and we went to battle. So let you and I alone fight together for the rule of the Indians."

219 When Poros heard this, he promised to fight him in single combat, deeming Alexander's body unequal to his own. For Poros was five cubits tall, while Alexander, three cubits. They faced one another in battle and both armies looked on and watched who would win. And Poros' army made a riotous commotion and Poros was startled and turned around to learn the reason for the shouting and unrest of the cavalry. Meanwhile, Alexander ran and sprang upon him and stuck his sword into his bowels; and thus he slew the giant, arrogant King Poros. And he knocked the fleshy heap off the horse. When the Persians and Alexander's Macedonian troops saw this, they leaped about in joy upon seeing their king so mightily and nobly conquer his opponent in the arena.

220 Then the satraps and the troops started to attack and fight one another, and Alexander said to them, "Wretched

and foolish Indians, why are you battling and fighting after the death of your king?" And they answered: "So that we be not enslaved." The king said to them: "Stop fighting, and go back to your city, free and fearless men. For it was not you who dared and presumed to make war on my armies, but it was Poros who fought with me. Now go back to your land and hold it in freedom." He said this knowing that his army was not equal to fighting with the Indians. And he ordered that Poros be buried as a king. And taking all his splendid possessions, gold and silver and splendid jewels, he journeyed straight to the Oxydarkes— not that they were a numerous or warfaring people but because they were gymnosophists,[1] who lived under huts and in caves. 221

And when they learned that Alexander had come to their land, they sent their noble philosophers to take him this letter, which Alexander took and read through. It went thus: "We the Brachmans, gymnosophists, send greetings to Alexander, the noble and mighty. Know that you shall find nothing to take away from us. But if you wish to take what we have, there is no need for bravery or battle for this. Rather come to us in love; perhaps you will learn who we are. For as a result of the guidance of Providence above, victory in war comes to you; while to us, this love of learning." 222

Upon reading this,[1] Alexander went to them in peace, and saw all the gymnosophists living under huts and in caves. And the women and children had been taken away and left with the flocks. He asked one of them, "Do you not have graves?" And he replied: "This place we live in is my grave. I shall lie here in the earth and bury myself in the sleep of those who dwell under the earth. For, in dying, I shall dwell in eternal sleep." And he said to another, "Who are the more numerous, the dead or the living?" And he replied: "The dead are more numerous. But you must not count what no longer exists; those who are seen are more numerous than those who are no longer visible." 223

121

And he asked another, "Which is more powerful, death or life?" And he said, "Life." The king asked, "Why?" "For the rising sun casts the strongest rays on earth, and in setting in the evening, is seen to be weakest." And he asked another, "Which is there more of, land or sea?" "Land; for the sea itself is set upon land." And he asked another, "Of all the animals, which is the cleverest?" And he replied, "Man." "Why is this?" "Ask yourself," he replied, "for see how many animals you have brought along with you in order to carry off all the other animals you capture." And the world conqueror did not get angry, knowing those who were speaking. And he asked another, "What is a king?" And he said, "An excess of greed, corrupt force, bold daring, a momentary success." And to another, he said, "Which is first, night or day?" And he replied, "Night." "Why is this?" And he said: "For he who is born grows in the dark of the womb, then comes forth to reach light." In turn, he asked another, "To whom can we not lie, but must speak truly?" And he replied: "To God. For we cannot lie to him who knows everything, that is, God." And he said to another, "Which is the best side, the left or the right?" And he replied, "The left." And he asked, "Why?" And the other replied: "For, in the first place, the sun climbs from the left to the right. And we mate with women from the left. A woman nurses by giving the child the left breast first. And we lift and carry the gods on the left shoulder. And so, too, you kings carry your royal scepters in your left hand." He asked another, "Who shall conquer all human races?" He replied, "Death. For it is violent and cruel towards all." And Alexander said, "At what things does God get angry?" He replied, "At the iniquity of the rich and the pride of the poor." He asked, "What is the sweetest thing in creation?" The answer, "Love from the heart." "And what is the most bitter?" "Envy and hate." When he had thus questioned each man, he said, "All of you together, ask me for whatever you like." They all cried out, "Give us immortality, that we might not die." And Alexander said, "I do not have that power, for even I am a mortal man." And they said: "And since you are mortal, why do you wage so many wars and cause so much suffering and spill so much blood that you might willfully have the possessions of all? And where will you take all this? Are you not going to leave it in turn to others?" The king said to them: "This is not determined by us but by Providence above, so that we are servants of its command; for the sea does not move if the wind does not blow, and trees do not stir if the air is still. Man achieves nothing unless he executes the will of Providence. And even if I wished to stop making war, the master of my behavior would not let me. For, if we all behaved the same way, the world would be idle and empty. There would be no navigation on the ocean; houses would not be built; marriages would not be consummated; there would be no children born. For a great many men have been ruined by my wars and have lost all their possessions; yet others have become prosperous on the riches of others. For all men grasp at everything, and in turn we leave it all behind to others; and there is nothing (permanent) anywhere." Alexander spoke thus and went on his way, undergoing many hardships in passing through impenetrable and untrodden places. And he was not a little troubled. Then, he wrote Aristotle a letter[1] about these happenings 224 that went thus: "King Alexander greets Aristotle, his teacher. We have deemed it very important to relate to you the marvelous and wonderful things that happened to us in the land of India. For we reached the Prasiakan[2] city which appeared to us to be the capital of India; and reaching it we occupied a conspicuous promontory of the Indian Ocean. And with a few men, I headed for the aforementioned places; and we searched and found fish-eating people with the forms of women feeding there. And I called some of them to me, and I found that they spoke a barbarian tongue. And I asked about the region; and they pointed out an island to me which we all saw in the middle of the sea, on which, they said, was the very ancient tomb of some king, where there was a great deal of gold which had been dedicated. And I was very eager to cross to the island, but the barbarians savagely resisted us. Then they withdrew and disappeared. And they left their boats, of which there were twelve. And although things were so, my good friends Phidon and Hephestion and other friends did not let me take the chance of crossing. My companion Phidon resisted especially, saying, "Instead, let me board that ship first and go see the island; then I will send you my boat. But you should not undergo any peril before I do; for if Phidon perishes, many other friends will be found for you; but if Alexander perishes, the whole world is ruined." And I was persuaded by him and permitted him to cross first with those twelve boats, in which 100 men embarked. The sailing was easy and they drew near to the island, for the evil barbarians had said it was an island, but it was a whale. And still they fearlessly got out and set and tied the boats with ropes as on an island. And after they had arrived and prepared passageways for the boats, they hauled the boats by rope into the lake-shaped place and came out where we could see them. And after an hour had gone by, all of a sudden, the beast plunged into the depths of the sea. We shouted out, but the creature disappeared; and the men perished, along with my friend. And I was deeply upset over the occurrence. We looked for the barbarians, but could not find them. And we stayed eight days on the promontory. On the seventh, we saw the beast; it had tusks[3] on it. And as many of the nobles were hurrying us, we passed on to the city of Prasias, and many marvelous and wonderful things were seen, which must be related to you; for we saw various beasts and the natural phenomena of the region and varieties of serpents. But what was most marvelous of all was the declining and sudden disappearance of the sun and the moon; and our way was suddenly blocked out. I must tell you about each of these things, venerable guide and teacher. After we had conquered Darius, the king of the Persians, and had subdued his men and taken them in our power, we went on and traveled through the whole land, seeing the wonderful things he ruled. For there was much gold and silver, and golden urns decorated with various precious stones; each urn held ninety servings. And there were many other wonderful sights. Starting from there, we traveled into the Caspian gates. And just as the tenth hour was beginning, the trumpets announced dinner at the ninth hour of night. For it was right that the traveling last five hours into the night and the remaining six hours be spent in bed at rest.[4] And with the rising of the sun, the trumpeters announced the fourth hour. And the preparation of the armies was so complete that each individual was equipped with boots, leather leg protectors, and coverings for the thighs; and they covered their bodies with chest armor. Since the residents of the region had told me earlier about the snakes killing people on the road, I had it announced to the people and made sure that no one was without his outfit, so that no harm befall him. And after we had traveled our endless way for twelve days, we came to a city in a river; and we wanted to camp on the sandy area near the river. And there was a reed in the city, thirty cubits in circumference,[5] from which all the buildings of the city were made. And the city did not stand on the ground but on these reeds. And there were boats on the river; and upon examining them, we saw that they had been made of boards of these reeds for protection. And then I ordered the army to camp there; and since we reached that place at the third hour of day, we walked about. And coming to the river, we found that the water was more bitter than hellebore. And when our men wanted to cross to the city, hippopotami rose and seized the men. And after that we had to get out of that place altogether. And the trumpet sounded and we moved on from the sixth to the eleventh hour, so deprived of water that I even saw soldiers drinking their own urine.

125

And then lo, we were passing through swamps and endless water and came accidentally to a place where there was a lake and trees bearing fruits of all kinds. Coming there, we assembled together, and found sweet water, which surpassed the sweetness of honey. And as I was rejoicing greatly with my friends, we found atop the promontory these words written, "Sesonchousis, ruler of the world, set up this monument for those who sail through the Red Sea." I ordered then that the army camp there and prepare for bed; and we sounded the trumpet for dinner. After this a fire was laid as a defensive precaution, as was our custom, and we went to sleep. And about the third hour of the night when the moon was bright, all the beasts of the forest came and collected at the mentioned lake to drink water. And among them there were scorpions a cubit long,[6] and sand burrowers, some white, others red, and a great fear gripped us. And the sudden cries and lamentation of men and youths dying affected us greatly. And four-legged animals began to come to the lake to drink water as was their custom. And among them were lions larger than bulls in our land, and great rhinoceroses came forth from the forest of reeds. So, too, boars larger than lions, with teeth a cubit long; and lynxes, leopards, and tigers, and scorpions, and elephants, and wild oxen, and bull elephants and barefooted men with six feet; and dog partridges and many other kinds of wild animals; and we could not resist feeling a terrible horror. And we drove certain of them away with iron weapons and we set fire to the woods. And the serpents ran into the fire. And there were those we stamped on and killed with our swords, but most of them were burnt; and this lasted until the sixth hour of the night, when the moon set. Shaken by fear and terrible dread, we stood wondering at their varied forms. And suddenly a wild animal came that was larger than any elephant, called a unicorn;[7] and it wanted to attack us. And I ran back and forth and beseeched my brave companions to make fires and protect themselves lest they meet a horrible death.

126

And the beast in its eagerness to hurt the men ran and fell into the flames. From there he ran into the army, killing twenty-six men at once. And some of our other brave men struck down and slew the one-horned beast. And 1,300 men were hardly able to drag him away from the place. And with the setting of the moon, suddenly night foxes ran out of the sand and they were five cubits long; and others were eight cubits long. And a few of them destroyed many of our men. A horde of crabs ran out of the lake and they destroyed my arms carriers, my fire pots, and all my tents. And there were bats larger than pigeons that had teeth like man's. Perched near the lake were owls which we hunted and of these we made a great dish for ourselves. They never attacked humans nor did they dare to approach the fire. And when it was day, these animals all went away. Then I ordered that the local guides, of whom we had fifty and who had led us to those evil places, be tortured and taken and thrown into the river. And we collected our things, and moved on twelve miles. And crossing through the desert, we came to and took the usual[8] road which leads to the city Prasias. And continuing on for a few days, we came to a very small town and I wanted to give my brave men five-days' rest. On the sixth day, about the sixth hour, after we had prepared and arranged everything for leaving, this is what was seen up in the sky. It was the third day of the month of Navasard.[9] First, there was suddenly a terrible wind which blew so hard it knocked down the altars and tents of the army; and we who were on foot were thrown to the ground. And I immediately ordered that the tents be set right and the other things be reinforced. And while we were getting organized, a cloud happened to come over; and it became so dark that that we could not even see one another. And after the cloud disappeared, the sky darkened and thickened without cause; then we saw in the sky a great wind and various things coming. And on the ground before us for ten stadia we saw all the clouds heaped together, and then again they quickly turned red. And this happened for three days. And for five days the sun disappeared, and there was much snow. It happened that the soldiers who dared go out were buried upright. As a result of this, more than seventy perished in the snow. And when the sun rose, we had lost many possessions and many of our men. And the fields rose three cubits from the ground on account of the accumulation of the snow. After thirty days, when the road became readily passable, we turned and went on. Five days later, we attacked and conquered the capital city of the Indians, Prasias, along with Poros and those who were with him, and the plentiful goods of all of them, about which you have been written. And after this, I put back in proper order the things around me. And the Indians of their own accord assembled together and said to me: 'Great King, you shall take cities and kingdoms and mountains and nations to which no living person has reached and attained. After this absolutely nothing exists worthy of your greatness. Tell us where, and all the men that there are in these little towns will come to you; and nowhere is more gold than there is here.' And I praised them and approved saying, 'Because I have come upon many wonderful things in my travels, if you know of any fable or wonder worthy of a king's attention, point it out to me.' And men came from the little towns and said, 'King, we have something wonderful that is worthy of showing you. For we shall show a plant that talks like man.' And I immediately ordered that they be beaten for tricking me; but nevertheless, I thought it important to find out. And going on twelve-days' journey from there, we came to a village which was said to be the end and southern boundary in the East. And beyond this, there is nothing, they said, but beast-infested wilderness, where no one of us may go. And when we reached the place, they took us into a garden. For the village was covered not by stones or by bricks but by trees, because of the sun and the moon. And in the middle of the park, as if for their protection, there was

128

the sacrificial shrine to the sun and the moon. And there were two trees, both very similar, which were the same size as the cypress trees at home. And all about were the aforementioned trees which are called 'myrabalanos'[10] in Egypt. And the fruit too was similar. And they called upon the male for advice for men, and the female for women. And the name of the male was the Sun, and the female, the Moon, which they call in their own language, 'mouthouam avousa.'[11] And these trees were covered with the skin of various animals, the male of the males, and the female of the females. And they had neither iron, copper, tin, nor clay for making anything. And I asked, 'Of what are these the hides?' And they replied, 'Of lions and leopards.' And it was not allowed to have any tomb there, except that of the Sun and of the Moon. And they used the hides of animals as their garments. And I asked questions to find out the reason for the animals. And they said, 'When it becomes light at the hour the sun rises, a voice comes from those trees; also, when the sun is in mid-sky and again when it is getting ready to set: these three times.' And they said the same is true about the moon. And they also said that as long as the sun moves and shines, they (the trees) give oracles; and when the moon appears, the same was true for it. And people who appeared to be priests came to me and said, 'Enter with a pure heart and make reverence.' And my friends, Parmenion, Krateron, Oullon, Machitas, Thrasileonta, Sachaona, and his companion, Theodechton, Niokle, ten men in all, were going in with me. And the priest said, 'King, it is not right to bring iron into the shrine.' So I ordered my friends to leave their swords outside the enclave. And from the army 300 unarmed men came with me. I ordered all the men who were with me to look around and see lest perhaps there be someone up on the trees. And they looked and searched and said there was no one. I called to me those Indians who had come with me that I might get a translation from them. 'I swear by Olympian Aramazd, Ammon, Athena,

all victory-giving gods, that I am not going to kill you.'
And simultaneously with the setting of the sun, a voice in
the barbarian Indian tongue came from the trees; and it
was not translated for us. I summoned to me some Indians,
but they refused to translate for me what the trees had
said. For they were afraid of me and did not wish to reveal
it. And I became concerned and laid hold of them and
took them aside; and the Indians whispered this in my ear,
'Know, King, that soon you are to be slain by your own
men.' When these heavenly signs were revealed and the
moon was about to disappear in the east, those who were
with me wanted to get another oracle at night. And having
reflected upon my fate, I went within and asked entreat-
ingly if I might return to my mother, Olympias, and to my
good friends, alive. And again while my friends were there,
when the moon rose, the tree made the same sound, saying
approximately this in Greek: 'Alexander, you are to die
in Babylon. You shall be slain by your own men, and you
may not return to your mother, Olympias.' And my
friends and I were dumbfounded. I wanted to donate
beautiful wreaths to the gods, but the priest said: 'It
is not proper to do this. But if you insist, do as you
please, since there are no laws written for a king.' And
since I was very sad and vexed with matters, Parmenion
and Philip beseeched me to sleep and to get ready for
the morning. And since I did not care to do so, I rose in
the morning with the rising of the sun, and with ten friends
again entered the temple; and I left them to one side so
that no one in the army would know my business.[12] And
coming to the tree with the priest, I put my hand on the
tree and asked, 'If the years of my life are finished, I
wish to learn from you whether I shall return to Macedon
and greet my mother and wife, Roxiane, and shall thus
depart.' And at the same time as the sun rose and cast its
light on the edge of the tree, a voice became sharp and
clear, and it said, 'Alexander, the years of your life are
ended; and you are not to have your wish of reaching your

mother, Olympias; instead, you are to perish in Babylon and are not to enter Macedon. The reason? You deprived many men of the sight of their mothers and cities and countries and friends. And just as one sows, so in fact shall he reap. And a little while later, your mother and your wife are to be cruelly slain by their own people; and your sister, by your own family. And do not importune me about this, for you shall be heeded no more even though you pleadingly petition me.' Then I left there about the first hour; and when one day had come and gone its way, I summoned all the troops and spoke to them together about their wishes. And traveling fifteen days, I soon reached the city of Prasias; and they sent to the neighboring cities to find out what strange things were being experienced from the things brought from the South. They brought before me fish skins and those of leopards, and fangs larger than three cubits; 'ouzomoures' six cubits long, weighing a talent and 'ioulidas'[13] weighing two talents, and other fish fangs a cubit long, which they had fashioned into scabbards for swords. They brought forth and offered me shellfish along with all the other things. One was saffron colored and held six portions, and it was very marvelous to see; and the other held four portions; and there were others, that held a portion apiece. And there were thirty saffron sponges and fifty green ones.[14] And moving on from the city of Prasias, we have come and reached Persia, the kingdom of Šamiram.[15] I thought it important to tell you these things. Farewell."

When Alexander had written this letter to Aristotle, he   225
rushed his army to the palace of Šamiram, for he wished to see it since it was famous throughout Hellas and the entire world. For the city was walled around by natural rocks; it was three stadia long and wide, and it was enclosed by 120 doors. The outside of these doors was decorated with iron and copper, for there was much iron in their land. And the whole city was made up of stone residences. And a woman, who was endowed with infinite beauty, ruled the

city. Her husband was middle-aged; and she was the mother of three children. And the name of the queen of Šamiram was Candace.

226 Alexander in turn sent her a third letter, which went thus: "King Alexander greets Queen Candace, who is in Meroë, and the kings under her command. I reached Egypt and heard about you there from the priests while I was visiting your graves; and the characteristic of the latter made it clear that at a certain period you ruled Egypt and Ammon led your armies. And after a short time, there was an oracle from Ammon, and you turned back to your land. Because of this, I have written to you that you bring the altar and statue of Ammon to the frontier so that we might sacrifice to him. If you wish, come with him, too, so that we might, without delay, meet in Meroë and deliberate together.[1] Let us know what seems best for us."

227 And then Queen Candace wrote him a letter which went thus: "Queen Candace of Meroë and the kings under her command greet Alexander. At that time an oracle came from Ammon to march upon Egypt, but now one comes telling me not to move personally from my land[1] and to let no one attack me and, in fact, to wreak vengeance on those who attack us and to deal with them as we do with enemies. And do not be mistaken about our color. For in our souls we are lighter than the white men amongst you. And there are enough of us to hold out for time without end. We have eighty squadrons ready for those who come to do us harm. You would do right in glorifying the great god, Ammon. My messengers are bringing to you from us round bricks, 500 young Ethiopians, and 200 parrots; and for Ammon, our god, who presides over the boundaries of Egypt, this crown made of pierced emeralds and pearls; 50 necklaces and 10 saters more of whole pearls and whole emeralds, and 80 ivory dishes and chests. And with my possessions are being sent a variety of beasts from us: 360 elephants; 300 leopards; 13 rhinoceros; 4 panthers; 90 man-eating dogs with cages; 300 fighting bulls; 90 elephant

132

tusks; 300 leopard skins; 7,500 ebony Indian staffs. Now send anyone you wish to take these things forthwith. And write us when you have conquered the whole world."

When Alexander received and read this, he sent Kleomes, 228 the governor of Egypt, to go get these things. And he went to the lady. And when Candace heard about Alexander and how he really vanquished barbarian nations and overpowered so many great kings, she summoned from amongst the people there a Greek painter. And she ordered him to go to Alexander as though to welcome him, and, without letting it be known, to paint him; and then to come back and give the painting to Lady Candace. And when he had done this, she put it in a secret place.

And then this happened. The son of Candace whose name 229 was Candaules rode with a few horsemen to the tent of Alexander. And the men standing guard there took him and led him to the Savior Ptlomeos,[1] who was second in command, for the world conqueror was asleep. Ptlomeos asked him, "Who are you?" And he replied, "The son of Candace the Queen." "And what are you doing here?" And he said, "I was coming with my wife and a few men to perform the annual sacrificial rite among the Amazons. But when the king of the Bebrycians saw my wife, he came forth with a great army and carried her off and slew many of my soldiers. Now I shall return and, once I have gotten more soldiers, shall defeat Bebrycia." And when Ptlomeos heard this, he arose and went in to Alexander and woke him up and told him all that he had heard.

And when the king heard this, he stood up and taking his 230 crown, crowned Ptlomeos and put his cloak about him, and said to him: "Go forth as though you were Alexander, and say, 'Summon Antigonos, my comrade in arms,' and when I come, tell me the story; and after relating this, we shall take counsel about these things, and give me your advice." And Ptlomeos went forth and when the troops saw him, they reflected and said, "What is the keen-witted Alexander planning?" But when Candaules, the son, saw him in the royal dress, he was afraid that he might order him put to death; for he thought it was Alexander.

231 And Ptlomeos said, "Let someone call Antigonos, my comrade in arms." Alexander appeared and Ptlomeos said to him: "Antigonos, this is the son of Candace, the queen; his wife has been seized by the king of the Bebrycians. What do you advise me to do?" And he said, "My lord Alexander, I advise you to ready the army for war against the Bebrycians, that we might rescue his wife and hand her over to him in honor of his mother." And Candaules rejoiced upon hearing this. Ptlomeos said: "If this is what you want, Antigonos, do it. As my adjutant, order that the troops be readied." And they prepared to execute the command of Ptlomeos as if it were Alexander's.

232 They reached these regions after one day. Antigonos, who was Alexander, said: "Let us not appear to the Bebrycians by day lest the king be alerted and slay this fellow's wife before the battle. What glory will victory hold for us if Candaules loses his wife? Let us rather attack the city at night and set fire to the houses. Thus the crowds themselves will hand the woman over to us, for our dispute is not over the kingship but over the demand for the wife." And when Antigonos had spoken thus, Candaules fell before him and said: "Bravo for your great thoughts, wise Antigonos. Could you by any chance be Alexander and not Alexander's adjutant?"

233 Now they entered the city at night; and while they were asleep, they lit a fire outside the palace. And they awoke and asked what the cause of the fire was; and Alexander ordered that Candaules shout back, "A very mighty king commands you to release that woman before I set fire to your entire city." And they who were first aroused woke all the others. They went to the palace of the king and by the force of the crowd opened the palace and took the woman out of the bed of the king and gave her to Candaules, and they slew the king.

234 And Candaules was very grateful for the counsel and con-

sideration of Alexander. He returned from there to Alexander's army, embraced him, and said, "Antigonos, entrust yourself to me, and come to my mother so that I might present you royal gifts." And he smiled and answered, "Ask the king to let me go, for I too would like to see that city." And Alexander, actually Ptlomeos, said to Candaules, "I wish to send a letter of greeting to your mother, the queen." And Candaules asked the king for Antigonos so that he might take him to his mother and send him back with regal gifts. Alexander, actually Ptlomeos, said: "Take Antigonos as my messenger and send him safely back just as you yourself are going safely to your mother, accompanied by your wife who has been freed from the king of the Bebrycians by your bravery." And he said: "Mighty King, I swear by all the gods, and upon your head and my mother's destiny, that I shall take this man with me as if he were you yourself, the world conqueror; and I shall send him back to you with great honor and with royal gifts."

And Alexander set out with a great force with him; and he took beasts of burden and wagons for the journey. And as he went, he marveled at the various crystal-bearing mountains of the land, which reached as high as the clouds of heaven, and at the tall trees, laden with fruit, not as in Hellas, but each individually worthy of wonder. For the apple trees were golden-colored and their fruit, when it ripened, was like the cucumbers in Hellas. And there were bunches of grapes which cannot be described in writing, and pomegranates which were bigger than watermelons. But there were great numbers of serpents wrapped around the trees, and lizards even bigger than the serpents. And there were monkeys not at all smaller than barbarian wild animals, or Greek bears; and there were many other animals of various colors and of novel shapes. And certain places were wondrous and had a godly quality, and there were deep caves with rocky descents. Candaules said: "Antigonos, these places are called the dwelling place of gods; and the gods

235

are often seen in these caves, reclining on couches, when a king invokes them. And so if you want to, on your return, take your dedicatory offering and sacrifice it on the spot, and they will appear to you." Candaules spoke thus, and they continued the journey.

236 Now they reached the palace; and his mother and brothers went to meet them. And when they were about to embrace him, Candaules said: "Brothers, do not embrace me without first greeting him who has been my savior and the benefactor of my wife: Antigonos, the messenger of the great King Alexander." To this, they said, "What salvation did he offer you?" And when he had related everything, both the abduction of his wife by the Bebrycians and this man's help, then his mother and brothers hugged and embraced him and they prepared a splendid feast in the palace.

237 And the next day, Candace appeared in her royal crown, revealing her very great height and her godly face and it seemed to Alexander that he was seeing his mother, Olympias. And he saw the palace with its gleaming golden roofs and stone walls. The coverlets were Chinese woven work, decorated with gold. And there were thrones standing on onyx and beryl, and their seats had been reinforced by leatherbound fastenings. And there were tables produced from ivory material, and there was the offering of work made of turquoise. And the columns were Numidian, the capitals of which were of shiny black Indian wood. And there were votive statues of men made of fine copper; and these could not be counted because of their great number. And there were chariots armed with scythes, together with their horses and drivers, fashioned from purple stone; and they gave you the impression they were charging off to the races. And carved from the same stone there were elephants trampling the enemy and wrapping their trunks around their opponents. And there were also altars with columns carved from a single stone. And there were statues of barbarian gods displaying their blood-red countenances to the onlooker. And high-rising beams formed a covering like

plane trees that had naturally grown tall. And there was water that had the color and sparkle of gold and flowed like a river and seemed to be another Pactolos. And each one of the trees, planted in rows, had on its branches ripe, delectable fruits. And Alexander was astonished and filled with wonder upon seeing these things.

And he was the fraternal[1] dinner guest of Candaules. 238 Candaules beseeched his mother and bade her give the messenger such gifts as she judged proper and thus send him off.

And the next day, Candace took Antigonos and showed 239 him the bright rooms, made of a clear-colored stone, that were so bright and shiny because of the marble planks, that it seemed as if the sun were inside the walls. And in one, there was a great altar made of indestructible woods; and it could not be burnt by fire. And a house had been built, the foundation of which was not set on the ground but upon great square cut boards set with wheels, and it was drawn by twenty elephants. And wherever the king went to make war on a city, he lived in it.

And Alexander said to the queen, Candace, "All this would 240 be wonderful even if it were in the land of the Greeks and not in your country." Candace was incensed and she said, "What you say is true, Alexander." And he was caught unaware at thus being addressed by name, and he turned aside. And she continued, "Why did you turn aside upon being called Alexander?" And he said, "My lady, my name is Antigonos, Alexander's messenger." The queen said: "Although you are called Antigonos among my people, you are King Alexander. And now I shall prove it to you." And she took his hand and led him in to her chamber, and she brought and showed the portrait to him. And she said to him: "Do you recognize your likeness? Now, why are you trembling? Why are you disturbed—you who destroyed the Persians and conquered the Indians and have undone the might of the Medes and Parthians? Now without fighting or force, you have fallen into the hands of

Queen Candace. Hereafter, Alexander, know that no matter how smart a man appears to be, there may be another wiser and more intelligent than he."

241 At this, Alexander got very angry and gnashed his teeth. "Why get angry? Why gnash your teeth?" continued Candace. "What can you do to me—you who are so great a king?" And he said, "I am gnashing my teeth in horror and am truly angry that I do not have my sword with me." The lady said, "And suppose you had it, what could you do?" And he replied: "Rather than obey you, I would slay you first, so that there would be no trace of you left, and then I would kill myself." And she said: "What kind of brave and kingly thoughts are those? But don't be afraid, Alexander. For as you once saved my child and his wife from the Bebrycians, so, too, shall I save your life by not telling the barbarians that you are Alexander. For if they find out that you are that Alexander, they will savagely put you to death; for you have killed Poros, and the wife of my youngest son is the daughter of Poros. Therefore, be called Antigonos, for I shall keep your secret in the depths of my heart."

242 Having said this, she went outside with him and said: "My son, Candaules, and my daughter, Marpesga,[1] if you had not come upon Alexander's army at the opportune time, I would not have received you back here again nor would you have found your wife. Now come; let us deal properly with Alexander's messenger and offer him gifts as is fitting." And her second son, Karagos,[2] said, "Mother and Queen, Alexander saved my brother and his wife; give him now whatever you want." But the third son said: "Lady Mother, my wife is in mourning for her father who was slain by Alexander. And now she wishes to cause the Macedonian sorrow. And since we have his messenger in our hands, let us kill this man, Antigonos." She asked: "And what good does that do you, my son? It makes no difference to Alexander if we kill this man, for he has many other servants beside this one." And Candaules said: "Be-

138

sides, this man was my wife's and my savior, and I am obliged by my oath to send him back safely from here to the king. But if this is to be the way it is to be, and we are going to fight one another because of this man, it is not my wish. But, if this is your will, you shall find me ready."

And Candace fearing lest her children fight, took Alexander aside, alone, and said: "Alexander, you have been resourceful in all matters; and yet you cannot find a single reason so that my sons might not fight because of you."[1]   243

And Alexander said: "Karagos and you, Candaules, it makes no difference to Alexander if you kill me here. For messengers are not precious things to kings, but rather are superfluous to him in the waging of war. So if you slay me here, Alexander has other messengers; but if you wish to capture Alexander, your enemy, easily through me, promise to give me a share of the gifts here so that I shall come and stay amongst you; and I shall persuade the king to come to you under the pretext that you wish to offer him in person the gifts which you are preparing. Then you will have him in your hands and can avenge yourselves. And once you have agreed to this, you will put an end to your grievances."   244

The brothers agreed. And Candace marveled and wondered at Alexander's intelligence; and she said to him, apart: "Alexander, if only you, too, were my son; for through you, I would rule all nations. For not by war alone have you subdued the world and its people, but by great wisdom. So come now, and be safe from them. It is Candace's great duty to keep this secret. But I advise you hereafter not to trust yourself to be your own messenger, unless you want to be like those who are trying to commit suicide."   245

And a few days later, at the time of his leave-taking, Candace gave him regal gifts: a crown of adamant worth many talents, and an amice made of precious stones of onyx and turquoise, and a cloak that shone like stars, entirely purple   246 and made of gold threads. And with such honor, she sent him off under the protection of her soldiers.

247 And when the king had gone the indicated number of days, he reached those wonderful caves where Candaules had told him the gods congregate. He entered with a few soldiers, and he saw a starlit haze. And the roof-tops were shining as if lit by stars. The external forms of the gods were physically manifest and a crowd was serving in silence. At first he was frightened and surprised. But he stayed to see what would happen, for he saw some reclining figures, whose eyes were shining like beams of light. And there was one who said: "Glad greetings, Alexander. Do you know who I am?" He said, "No, my lord." The other said: "I am Sesonchousis, the world-conquering king who has joined the ranks of the gods. But I was not so fortunate as you, for you will have an immortal name even after death." And I asked, "How is that, my lord?" He replied: "For although I conquered the whole world and subjugated so many peoples, nobody knows my name. But you shall have great renown for building in Egypt the city of Sk'andaria, which is dear to the gods, and also Souttloys, Ialan, Drauł, Łoudal. Now enter within and you shall see the creator and overseer of the entire universe."[1]

248 The king went within and saw a fire-bright haze and, seated on a throne, the god whom he had once seen being worshiped by men in Rokotide, that is, the lord Sarapis. He said: "How is this, O Lord, divine offspring of untainted nature? I saw you near the land of the Libyans seated on a throne, and now I see you here once again." And Sesonchousis, who was standing close to him, said to Alexander: "He is seen everywhere, though he is fixed in one spot; just as the sky is seen everywhere though it is set fast at a certain height in the firmament."

249 And Alexander said, "Lord, God, how many years shall I live?" And Sesonchousis said: "It is well for mortal man not to know when he is to die. For in waiting for that one day, he is dead from the day he has found out. While to be

140

ignorant of it brings the secret forgetfulness of not remembering that one is ever going to die. Still, the city you are building will be celebrated and famous to all men, food giver and nurse of the whole world. And many kings shall come to your feet to make reverence as to the gods; and you shall live there upon dying and not dying, for the city which you are building shall be your grave."

When the herald had so spoken, Alexander left. He took his men and continued the journey to be made. His satraps met him, crowned him king, and gave him his royal robe. And he journeyed on to the Amazons. And when he approached that place, he sent them a letter which went thus: "King Alexander greets you Amazons. I think you know about the war against Darius and that from there we went to the Indians with our army. And we found there noble men who were their leaders and their kings and their gymnosophists. And we took tribute from them. We let them remain there on their own lands and put the country at peace. For this reason, they received us gladly, and they had sacrifices made on our behalf. On our way back from there, we have come to you. Now come to meet us, for we do not come to do harm but rather to visit the country and at the same time be of service to you. Farewell."

And when they received this, they wrote him: "The Amazonian nobles and the leaders of the army greet you, King Alexander. We are writing you so that you might be fully informed before you enter this region, lest you be forced to leave it ignominiously. In this letter, we now clearly inform you of the facts about our land and about us: that we are brave and noble people and that we live on the Amazon River, but on this side, on an island. It takes a year's journey to travel around it. And around it there is a river which has no beginnings; and there is one entrance. We 200,000 warrior virgins who have no experience of men live here, and there is no male amongst us. Our men live on the other side of the river. The state of the land is such that we live in happiness. And from year to year, we

250

251

252

141

have a ceremonial assembly, a collective celebration, when we sacrifice horses to Aramazd and Poseidon and Hephestion for thirty days. And then we cross to the other side of the river to the men and they mate with us in marriage, for thirty days. And those of us who wish to be violated cross over and live among the men; and they pass over to us all the females that are begotten when they reach seven years of age. And whenever an enemy army comes upon our land, more than 120,000 of us go to meet them on horseback, and the others protect the island. We advance to the borders, and the men draw up the rear behind us. And if anyone is wounded in battle, she is fed from the sacrificial altar of Aramazd; and everyone pays her homage for two days; and there is a memorial crown for her family. And whosoever falls in battle in the defense of this homeland, the close relatives receive a not insignificant compensation. And if any of the enemy crosses to the island, there is a prize for his defeat that comprises much gold and silver and an allowance of food for life. Thus we would all sacrifice ourselves for our country. And if we conquer the enemy or if they flee, shame comes and stays upon them, tracking them forever. But if they conquer us, it will be a victory over Amazonian women. So, watch out, King Alexander, lest this happen to you. We will crown you year after year for as long as you decree.[1] Now think this over and answer us. You shall find our army on your boundaries."

253   And when the king received and read the letter, he smiled broadly and wrote thus in return: "Alexander, king of all kings, greets you women of Amazon. We have conquered three quarters of the universe with heavenly assistance. And nowhere have we left a sign of defeat, but, in fact, have vanquished all. Now it is shameful for us to desist and not attack you with our army. So if you want to ruin and devastate your country, stay there on your boundaries. But, if you wish to live in your country and not experience warfare, cross that river and appear before us. And let your

142

men likewise draw themselves up in that plain. If you do this, I swear to you by my father, Aramazd, and Ares, and Hera, and Athena, the conqueror, not to take anything away from you. And I shall take, in soldiers, such tribute as you wish to give and shall not enter your homeland. So send us the number of horsemen you decide upon and we shall give each woman, each month, five golden minae, as well as other things. At the end of the year, they shall be released to their homeland; and you will send us others in exchange for them. Now take counsel and send us your answer. Farewell."

And having taken counsel, they wrote him an answer which went thus: "We Amazonian nobles and the leaders of the army received the orders of the autocratic King Alexander. We give you the right to come on through to us and to visit our country. And we are arranging to give you yearly one hundred talents of gold; and we have sent 500 of the bravest of us to come to your borders, bringing you gifts and 100 brave horsemen. They will remain among you for a year. And if any of them be defiled by a foreigner, she will be disgraced in the eyes of the law of her land. And let us know as to which ones will wish to stay with you and dismiss the others; you will get replacements. For we submit to you in your presence and from afar, as we have heard of your great virtue and might. For what are we against the whole world that you have traversed that we should stand apart in opposition to you? So it has seemed best to us to live in our land in obedience to you."

And having arranged this, he traveled to the land of the Parasangians.[1] And the soldiers became very lazy and indifferent to the prizes to be had. Aramazd did not stop raining for forty days, to the point that the braces of the shields were rotted by the water, and also the bridles of the horses. And the feet of many of the youths were soaked and sore because of being barefooted. And when the rain stopped, it became so hot that no one could bear it. And there were great thunderings and frequent flashes of

254

255

143

lightning, until here and there rumblings began spreading in the army about the things going on. And since they were planning to cross the river, he asked the residents about the size of the army of the king who was on the other side in the land of the Parasangians, which was near the Ocean. And the inhabitants of the country told him that he had 5,000 stall-fed elephants, and 10,000 chariots, and tens of thousands of men. When wise Alexander heard this, he pillaged along the river and the rest of the land of the Indians and, in this fashion, built altars and had his soldiers make burnt offerings to the gods.

256 And he received a letter from the philosopher Aristotle, which went thus: "Aristotle, greets you King Alexander. I do not know what to talk to you about first and what last, for Aramazd bears witness and so, too, Poseidon, that I first of all give thanks to all the gods everywhere for your fortunate and distinguished and celebrated accomplishments. For you have undertaken every contest, battle, and danger, and you have not been defeated in a single one. For even in the land of the Indians, you were exposed to a second very perplexing winter, and you came out of it. And if anyone could endure exposing himself to that same land, he would gain a reputation for noteworthy and celebrated and wonderful deeds. For the noble warrior is easily recognizable. In council, he is a Nestor; in military warfare, a brave Odysseus.[1] He has seen the lands of many men and learned their ways of thinking. I say this to you because your deeds have been accomplished at about the age of thirty. They say that Alexander, the Macedonian, has reached from the West to the East; and people from the West and people from the East, the Ethiopians and the Scythians, joyfully welcomed him. And others who thought of opposing you have beseechingly petitioned you to befriend them. Indeed, you are a godlike king. Fare thee well."

257 And he took his army and went to Babylon. And upon his arrival there, he was feted with great honor; and he

offered sacrifices to the gods and held a gymnastic contest and a musical one.

When these things had been done, he then wrote a letter to his mother, Olympias, about the things that had happened to him of which this is a copy.[1] And in sending this letter, he informed the queen, Olympias, of the things he had personally done; and he told her everything clearly and distinctly, detail by detail as follows: "I, the mighty king and sovereign monarch of three quarters of the world, send my most distinguished mother, Olympias, fond greetings. Let it be clear that I am sure that you are cognizant of what we have done from the outset right up to what took place in Asia, as I have written you of these things. And I have decided to inform you also about the journey to the upper regions. For I made still another trip, going toward Babylon and taking 150,000 trusted soldiers with me. And having reached Parasanges, I came to the pillars of Heracles, in ninety-five days.[2] For they say that Heracles set, as the boundary of the world, two columns, one of gold and the other silver; one, twelve cubits high, the other, two.[3] And since I did not believe that they were made solid, I decided to make a sacrifice to Heracles and then to pierce one of the columns. And I saw it was solid gold. I wanted to fill up the hole again, and the cavity was found to hold 1,500 gold miskals,[4] which is a kind of money. And from here, we went on through wild and rocky places, and because of the mist we were not able to see who the person next to us was. And we departed from these regions, and in seven days, we came to Parasanges. The river named Thermadon is there, which has its beginning and end in Pautos, a flat, open region with good roads. And the Amazon women live here, who exceed in size and beauty all other women. And they are virtuous and noble. They had flowered garments and wielded weapons with silver axes. There was no iron or copper there. They were endowed with skill and intelligence. And we camped our army near the river, since we could not cross to the other side where

145

the Amazon women dwelt, for the river was big and very deep, and had many wild animals and black rocks. And they crossed over and met us. And we took tribute from them and went toward the Red Sea, to a strait. On the right, there was a high mountain, and on the left, beat the sea. And having sacrificed ten horses to Poseidon, we rested on the second day and went on and came to the Atlas River. And here, neither sky nor the earth could be seen. And many peoples of many kinds lived there. We saw dog-headed men and headless ones[5] who had their eyes and mouths on their chests. And there were also those who burrowed holes, wild creatures who lived under the earth. And there was a land one-day's journey by ship from here. And upon sailing near the place, we found the city Areg.[6] It is my opinion that this is the one they call the city of bronze.[7] Its circumference is 120 stadia; and in it were fourteen towers built of gold and emerald, each of which had sixty steps.[8] And on top there was a chariot with horses of gold and emerald. It was not easy to see them on account of the fog. And the priest of the sun was an Ethiopian. And offering sacrifices to the sun because we had not found any light, we turned and went on from there. And Persian torch bearers preceded us, carrying lighted silver lamps. And we came to the river Tanaïs, which flows both to Asia and to Europe. And from there we moved on and came to the palaces of Xerxes and Cavos. We found fine houses full of gold and silver and many remarkable drinking cups and many other fine things. And there was a large house of many stories where the king himself used to receive oracles from the gods. It was said that, in it, a bird interpreted the omens in a human voice. For there was a golden bird cage in the middle of the ceiling, and in it was that bird which was about the size of a dove. They say that it interprets in a human voice to kings when it hears the sounds which pulse through it. And they said that it was very old. And I wanted to take it down to send it to you, but the priest said that it belonged to the voice. And in the palace at Šoš we also found a silver urn that held 360 measures, which we counted at the great banquet. In it, we also made sacrifices for our safety. And there was a large house in which was inscribed Xerxes' sea battle with the Athenians. And in the middle there was a throne of gold and, above it, a golden altar where they said the king received oracles from the gods, whenever a delegation came from somewhere. There too was the art of Glaukos—a harmonious lute that played by itself.[9] And around the throne, there was a goblet holder, sixteen cubits high with twelve steps; and, above it, there was a gold eagle with its wings spread out over the whole width of the goblet holder. And there was a seven-branched bough of pure gold, and a white plane and myrtle tree. And all these things were wrought with beautiful workmanship. Although I would write you more about these things, they were so numerous that we could not remember them all because of their great number. Farewell, my mother."

And he had written this letter to his mother, Olympias, while he was in Babylon and was preparing to quit his mortal life. And the evil spirit gave a great and clear sign, for this omen occurred. When one of the local women gave birth to a child, the upper part of its body, as far as the navel, was completely human and according to nature, but the lower extremities were those of a wild beast. And its general appearance was like that of Scylla except that it differed in the kinds of animals and in the great number of them. For there were the shapes of leopards and lions, wolves and wild boars and dogs. And these forms moved, and each was clearly recognizable to all. And the child was dead and his body blue. And immediately upon giving birth to the above-mentioned baby, the woman put it in the fold of her robe and hid it. And she came to the palace of Alexander, and told the chamberlain to announce her to the king, "for I have something of importance to show and tell him." And he happened to be resting in his room at midday. And when he awoke and heard from

259

147

the chamberlain about the woman who had come, he ordered that she be brought in. And when she entered, the king ordered those who were there to leave. And when they had gone out, she uncovered and showed him the marvel that had been begotten, saying that she herself had given birth to it. When Alexander saw it, he was filled with wonder and great amazement. And he called together the magi and the Chaldean sign-readers and ordered them to make a reading concerning it, promising them either death or harm if they did not tell the truth. And they were famous and widely reputed and the most learned of the Chaldeans. But the one who was more able in his art than all the rest happened not to be there. Those who were present said that Alexander was the greatest of men and the terror of his enemies and that he held sway over land and sea. And they said that the mighty and terrible monsters placed beneath the human body meant this: that he is to rule the mightiest men and that no one shall be mightier than he. And after they had explained how it was, they left him and went away. And after them, the other Chaldean returned from his trip and came to the king. And upon seeing the state of the omen, he gave a great outcry and rent his clothing and was greatly troubled and saddened at the transformation that was to befall the great king. And when the king saw that the man was so smitten by the happenings, he was greatly frightened; and he ordered him to explain frankly what the omen looked like. And he said this to him: "King, hereafter, you are no longer among the living; rather your body has left its mortal state. For such is the meaning of the marvelous omen." And Alexander asked him about these words. And the omen solver answered and said: "O bravest of all men, you are the human body, and the wild animal forms are the soldiers who are with you. If the human part of the body were alive and moving, as are the animals beneath it, you would have been destined to rule all men. But it is this very part that is dead; and the beasts are alive. So just as it has left its living state, so have you too departed to those who are no more. For example, the animals that are bound to the human body have no kind consideration toward man. In the same way, do those who surround you love you. And there will be many upheavals in the world when you depart; and those about you will fall out with one another and will bloodily slaughter one another." The philosopher spoke thus and left. And the Chaldean thought it best to burn the child.

When Alexander heard this, he was touched to the very heart and saddened. He said: "Aramazd, you have brought the fraudulent game to an end for me. So if such is your desire, take me, this mortal man, to you also." And this is what he meant: that Dionysos, when the evil deeds done him by those under his rule were revealed, was judged to be one of the gods. So, too, Heracles, since he had distinguished himself to the whole world, was considered in the same way, for his deeds, to be a companion[1] of all the gods. And his mother, Olympias, wrote many times to him about Antipater, saying that he had deeply humiliated and spurned and dishonored her because she was Alexander's mother;[1] and that Antipater was still doing as he pleased and was writing slanderous accusations about her. Because Olympias was once again complaining, Alexander wanted to cross to Epirus,[2] for he knew how to put an end to Antipater's hostility to his mother. And he sent forth and summoned Antipater to him from Macedon by sending Krateros. And since Antipater was aware of Alexander's cleverness, he plotted the death of the world conqueror to be administered by the soldiers, for he was afraid that some evil might befall himself. For he had heard and he bore in mind the fact that Alexander had grown very proud as a result of the successes that had befallen him. And he sent out and brought the gentian drug whose power he knew was very deadly. And he put it in the hoof of a mule[3] and he boiled it in order to be able to keep the strength of the drug alive. For no other dish, be it of copper or of clay, could support the strength of the drug,

260

261

but was broken by it. And he put it in an iron box, and gave it to Kasandros with instructions to discuss with Iollas, his brother, the administration of the drug.

262   And when Kasandros arrived in Babylon, he found Alexander making sacrifices and receiving foreigners. He spoke with Iollas who was Alexander's chief cupbearer. And it so happened that a few days earlier Alexander had hit him on the head with a club for some misdemeanor. Thus, since the boy was prone to anger, he gladly listened to the suggestion of committing the crime. And he took as his helper Mandios,[1] a Thessalonian, who was a friend of Alexander and his own lover. And this fellow considered it a criminal injustice that his Iollas had received a caning. So, of his own will and desire, he agreed that they would give him the poison to drink.

263   Meanwhile, Alexander was enjoying himself with his close friends and the Dionysian artists. For many had come to Babylon to crown Alexander ceremoniously and to take part personally in the ceremony because of the notable glories of the very happy king.

264   And then when he got up and wanted to go to rest, Medios came to him and beseeched him to come to his friends, telling him, "Your important friends are all gathered together and are awaiting you." He said this, and Alexander was persuaded by Medios' cunning. He went to the party.

265   And twenty men were gathered there: Perdikkas, Meleadros, Pithon, Leonatos, Kasandros, Pokestes, Ptlomeos, Lysimachos, Philip, Olkias, Eumenes, Philip the doctor, Nearchos the Crete, Heraclides, Europpeos, Ariston, Pharsalios, Philip who had mechanical skills, Philotas, Menandres, Dardana. Of these men, Perdikkas and Ptlomeos, Olkias and Lysimachos, Eumenes and Asandros did not know what had been planned. But all the others were associated in the act and in agreement with Iollas and Kasandros and had given their oath. For they longed for material possessions, and they were wary of Alexander; and in their

hearts, they were greatly dismayed by his overweening pride.

When the king had stretched out, Iollas offered him the drink. And then, those who were there behaved in this fashion. They busily added remarks to the conversation to draw out as long as possible the taking of the drugs.[1] Suddenly, Alexander cried out as though he had been hit in the liver by an arrow. For a short while, he controlled himself and, supporting the pain, went off by himself, bidding those who were there to drink. And they were very frightened, and then and there broke up the party and observed the turn of events. Alexander wanted very badly to bring up the wine and asked for a feather, for this is the way he used to do it. And Iollas contaminated it with the drug and offered it to him. Because of this, the drug overcame him all the more effectively, passing undiluted through the body. And Alexander was very ill and trying in vain to vomit, he passed the entire night in awful pain, in dolorous groaning, and in patient suffering. 266

And on the next day, he realized his bad state, for he was uttering indistinct and unclear sounds because his tongue was already growing stiff. He sent everyone out, so that he might be quiet and alone to talk about what he wanted to. And Kasandros conferred with his brothers, and at night, rushed off to the hills, boldly taking his cup from Iollas. For he had made a pact with Iollas that if the king died, he would be freed from all responsibility. And he sent it to his parent in Macedonia, having written to him in code that the deed was done. 267

And at nightfall, Alexander ordered everyone to leave the house. Among those he dismissed were Kombaphe and Roxiane, his wife. And from the house there was an exit[1] toward the river called the Euphrates, which runs through Babylon. He ordered it opened and that no one be at the places they customarily stood guard. And when it was the middle of the night, he got up from his bed, put out the light, and crawled on all fours toward the river. And he 268

151

saw his wife, Roxiane, advancing toward him. He had been planning to act in a manner worthy of his great courage. She followed his final journey in the dark. And Alexander, scarcely making a sound, would groan, and Roxiane was directed to the cry. And he stopped and was still. And his wife embraced him and said, "Are you abandoning and leaving me, Alexander, by committing suicide?" And he said: "Roxiane, it is a small deprivation for you that my glory be taken away from you. But still let no one hear about this." And he turned away from Roxiane and went back home in concealment.

269 And when it was day, he ordered Perdikkas and Ptlomeos and Lysimachos to come in. He told them that no one else should approach him until he wrote a will about his affairs. And they went out. And then he seated near him the will makers, Kombaphe and Hermogenes, who were young men. And Perdikkas thought that Alexander would leave all his goods to Ptlomeos because he had often spoken to him of Ptlomeos' lucky birth. And Olympias, too, had made it clear that Ptlomeos had been fathered by Philip. So he had made him promise privately that he would in turn be a recipient of Alexander's possessions at the time of the division of his goods. And when night fell, the secretaries began to write. And the king ordered that Perdikkas and Loukias and Ptlomeos and Lysimachos be summoned to him. And they came into the palace.

270 And suddenly a great shout arose from all the Macedonians. And they all rushed upon the palace saying that they would kill the guards unless they showed them their king. And Alexander heard the noise of the uproar and Perdikkas came and informed him of what the Macedonians were saying. He ordered that his couch be lifted and put in a place where the army might pass and see him and that the soldiers be brought in, clad in a single garment, and taken out the other door, so that they make no trouble amongst themselves and start fighting. The Macedonians entered and passed close by him and gave him encouragement.

And there was no one who was not grieved over what had happened to such a great and world-conquering king.

And one of them named Peukalaos, who was not unattrac- tive in appearance, but an ignorant country lad who did not command even a single platoon, stood close to the monarch and said, "O Alexander, Philip your father ruled Macedonia well." He changed languages and sadly continued in Macedonian: "Lo, you are abandoning us. And all of Macedon is lost by your dying. It is well for all us Macedonians to die with you who made your ancestral city worthy of Aramazd." And Alexander was saddened; and he stretched forth his right hand and clasped the hand of the Macedonian and very clearly acknowledged his entreaties, for the Macedonians were passing by. Once again he sent Perdikkas out and ordered Olkias to read the will he had had written with his very keen and perceptive wisdom. And this is the copy of the will.[1]

"King and monarch, Alexander, son of Ammon and of Olympias, greets the generals of the Rhodians, rulers of an intelligent people. Since you accept as your boundaries the pillars of Heracles, our forefather, who was destined to join the ranks of the gods, and since you have wished to be on friendly terms, we thought it right to write you about what we have decided because we have always considered you of all the Greeks the fitting custodians of my achievements; there is the second reason, too, that I love your city. Therefore, I am writing that the guards be removed from your city so that it may boldly preserve its freedom. Also, we wish that our splendid treasure be kept among you. For we know that city of yours is good and deserves being remembered. Therefore, we shall see to it that it is taken care of no less than one of our own cities, and as is worthy of us. We have boldly taken control of each country; starting first from our birthplace, we have willfully reached this point. And we invited the ruling kings first of all to send from the army 1,000 talents of gold to the Egyptian temple, for we also ordered that our body be taken there. And, we permit, too, that the formal arrangements be made however the Egyptian priest think best. And we ordered that Boeotian Thebes be built again and refurbished from the royal treasury. We have judged that they have suffered quite enough, and they have been adequately reproached and fittingly admonished for the wrongs they did me. And also let grain be given by the Macedonians to the Thebans until the people of the city prosper. And we ordered that you, too, be given for the refurbishing of your city 300 talents of gold and 40 warships, so that you might be strong and free, and also 20,000 measures of crops from Egypt every year as a gift. And land shall be measured and marked off for you so that you may for all time have sufficient crops for yourselves. And you shall want for nothing. And Ptlomeos who has been my bodyguard shall take care of you, too. And we have pointed all these things out so that he might do right by you. Now do not suppose that this legacy was bequeathed you in vain, for I have appointed overseers for your kingdom, and it is the overseers' duty to administrate according to my provisions.

273 We, King Alexander, son of Ammon and Olympias, appoint Arideos, the son of Philip, king of the Macedonians, for the present time. But should there be a son of Alexander from Roxiane, we shall make him king of the Macedonians and give him whatever name the Macedonians as a whole wish. But, if Roxiane's child be a girl, let the wisemen of the Macedonians elect and choose whomever they want as their king, if they do not want Arideos, Philip's son, to rule over them. And let him who shall be elected preserve the kingdom of the Argives; and let the Macedonians, together with their king, give tribute to the Argives as has been traditionally done. And especially let Olympias, Alexander's mother, live in Rhodes of the Theogians.[1]

274 King Alexander, son of Ammon and Olympias, designates as guardian of the entire kingdom of the Macedonians, Krateron and his wife, Kevane, the daughter of Philip,

the king of the Macedonians. Egypt goes to Ptlomeos, and let him be given as wife Cleopatra, the sister of Alexander, ruler of the brave. And let them bring forth Perdikkas as governor and guardian of the land of Babylon as far as Bactria. And let his wife be Roxiane, the wife of Alexander. And I shall order the guardians of the kingdom to make a golden tomb worth 200 talents, in which the body of Alexander, the world conqueror, is to be placed. And let the aged and feeble Macedonians be sent back to Macedon and Thessalonica and let each be given according to his deserts. And let there be a golden throne in Athens for the goddess Athena, who is the most beautiful of the virgins. And let the panoply of King Alexander be sent to Argos as a gift to Heracles, along with 150 talents of gold for the city. And let the tusks of elephants and snake skins and 100 golden bowls and 100 fine rings be sent to Delphi. And Perdikkas,[1] I leave as king of Egypt and the city of Alexandria, the capital I have built so that you may keep the city of Alexander under my own name, that Alexander might live on as king. Taxiades[2] is appointed to that kingdom of the Indians which is near the Hydaspes, the river of fish; Pithon, in charge of what has been designated; the Paraplenesians, to Oxydarkes, the Bactrian, the uncle of Alexander's wife, Roxiane; and to Philip goes Bactria, the lands of Šoš and the land of the Parthians to the South. And Olkias is appointed king of Lyria,[3] and I shall give him 500 horses from Asia to take with him. And with them, let Olkias build bronze statues of Alexander, Ammon, Athena, Heracles, Olympias, and Philip. And he should consecrate these in the Olympian shrine or wherever he wish. And let the guardians of the kingdom consecrate a statue of Olkias. And let Ptlomeos also dedicate in Egypt bronze statues to Alexander, Ammon, Athena, Heracles, Olympias, and Philip."[4]

And when all this had been done, Olkias came in and he gave him the letter to take to the Theban, Asmenos. And Olkias hastened to read what pertained to the region of

Thebes. Because he ordered the city of Thebes be rebuilt and did further benefactions, Ismenias, now rejoicing over the city, eagerly started celebrating.

276 And Alexander was anointed with a certain assuaging balm which Roxiane put on him, and he was protected from great pain. And a light sleep came. Because of this, the demise was deferred for five days. Alexander asked for water to rinse out his mouth. And once again, Iollas altered the cup with the drug and offered it to him. And he took it and rinsed out his mouth. And then and there, oppressed by his pains, he cried out loudly; and he gave up hope in life and in the vain futility of this world.

277 He summoned Perdikkas and Ptlomeos and Loukias and Lysimachos, the Macedonian princes, and spoke thus to them: "Men, I have given definite instructions about the kingdom. Olkias has been entrusted the Rhodians; let them do as he directs. And now I am taking care of the legacy of Perdikkas and Antipater." And Olkias then touched the hem of his garment and wailing loudly went out. And he called Lysimachos to him and said, "Go to Thrace and grieve not." And he, too, cried out and ran off. And he said to Ptlomeos seated near him, "And you, go to Egypt and you shall take care of our body." But he spoke softly to him so that no one might hear, for Ptlomeos too was overcome by tears, and he hid his face in his robe and secretly wept.[1]

278 But the illness was strengthening its hold upon the emperor, and he was no longer able thereafter to speak. And he suffered great distress and anguish, and he groaned: "Providence above, I entrust to your care the throne of my kingdom; for you are king of land and sea, ablest and strongest of all the gods and heroes. Hear me now, Heracles and Athena and all you creatures above." And hard pressed by his illness, he gave his ring to Perdikkas.

279 And Roxiane cried loudly and rent her clothing and wanted to fall at the feet of her husband, Alexander. And Alexander sobbed and groaned deeply and placed his hand

156

on her head. And he took her by her right hand and handed her to Perdikkas. And by a glance, he made it clear that he was entrusting her to his care. And as he was doing this, the malady was pressing hard upon him. At that time, Roxiane was standing on his right, and around the three were Perdikkas, Ptlomeos, and Loukias. And he gave up the ghost and they laid out his body.

And thus did Alexander, the world conqueror and great king, pass on to the gods, after having lived thirty-three years. And I do not think that they speak falsely who say that he is the son of Aramazd, nor do those who say he is Ammon's. For he surpassed by far the mortal measure in his character, sound thinking, righteousness; in restraint, generosity, and virtue. He won many wars, and accomplished everything himself, personally, and the facts themselves testify to this. 280

And Ptlomeos came to him and said, "Alexander, to whom do you leave your kingdom?" He replied, "To him who has the ability, the will power, the perseverance, and the power of accomplishment."[1] And just as he said this, a dark mist crossed the sky and a bolt of lightning was seen to fall from heaven into the sea and with it a great eagle. And the bronze statue of Aramazd in Babylon quivered; and the lightning ascended into heaven and the eagle went with it, taking with it a radiant star. And when the star disappeared in the sky, Alexander too had shut his eyes. 281

Meanwhile, the Persians were fighting, since they wanted to take the king to Persia and worship him together with the god Mithra. And the Macedonians wanted to take him to Macedonia. To this, Ptlomeos said: "There is an oracular shrine of the Babylonian god. I shall get an oracle from him as to where we should take the body of Alexander." And when he was asked, the god of the Babylonians answered thus: "I personally give you an order which is advantageous to you all. There is a city on the Nile,[1] near the streams of Oceanus, which has five very fertile kingly fields near the land of the Amazons; it is called Memphis. Take your 282 son who has become one of the gods there and put him to rest, for he, the horned king, has become a cause for rejoicing." Thus did the divine oracle answer.

283   And then[1] Ptlomeos took him to Egypt and made a leaden slab for him and poured upon him mnesiotas[2] honey and hipatic[3] aloe; and the body was embalmed with incense and oil and put upon a mule cart and taken to Egypt. And when they reached Pellas, the Memnians came forth with trumpeters to meet at the altars in their accustomed way. And they took him to Memphis near Sesonchousis, the world-conquering demigod. A voice issued forth saying: "Take him to his city which he himself built. For wherever that man's body be, that place shall have no surcease from war and from turmoil, for he is a child of war."

284   So at that time, Ptlomeos made a grave for him in Alexandria, which is still called Alexander's Body. And he put him there with splendid honor, since Alexander had requested that this be done.[1] For the city was called by his name and is destined to rule all others. A priest was appointed in the city for the great gods Sarapis and Apis; when he went out, he was to be adorned very splendidly in purple with a crown of gold and receive an annual[2] sum equal to a talent. And he would be inviolate and free from every obligation. This man would have this kind of honor, for he would exceed all mankind in nobility. And this gift would remain even for his children.

285   Alexander fought with many kings, and dying, left them behind him. For he lived thirty-three years. He started warring at eighteen and fought for seven years until he was twenty-five. And the other eight years, he lived in peace. And he was cut off in the middle of his days by the treachery of adversaries. He conquered many nations, twenty-two barbarian and twelve Greek. And he built twelve cities which still remain today, rich and complete and populated by countless people: Alexandria, which he built on the bullheaded horse; Alexandria Kattison; the

158

Alexandria for Poros; Alexandria of Undranikos;[1] Alexandria of Scythia; Alexandria of Mesopotamia; Alexandria on the Dklat' River; Alexandria of Babylon; Alexandria of Troy; Alexandria at Massagyrs; Alexandria near Xanthos, and Alexandria near Egypt.

This mighty and fortunate world conqueror, Alexander, 286 was born in the month of Tubi of the Egyptian calendar, on the first day at sunrise. And he came to his end on the fourth day of the month of Parmouphir, toward nightfall. And his army called that day sacred because of Alexander who died young. And this is the end of his life span, both of his birth and development, of his victory and his valor, his kingship and his world-wide rule; of his genius and his wisdom, his equity and justice, righteousness and virtue. This life that was directed by Providence above ended in man's common death.[1]

NOTES 🐝

U<small>NLESS OTHERWISE</small> stated, all references to the Greek versions, *A*
(Cod. Paris 1711 of the 11th century), *B* (Cod. Paris 1685, dated
1469), *C* (Paris suppl. 113, dated 1567), and *L* (Leidens, Vulc. 93),
are to *Reliqua Arriani, et Scriptorum de rebus Alexandri Magni
fragmenta: Pseudo-Callisthenis Historiam Fabulosam, Itinerarium
Alexandri,* Carolus Müller (Paris, 1846). The Latin of Valerius (*V*)
is also from the same text.

The Armenian printed text is Venice ms. 424, undated, and is
referred to as *P* (printed text). Other Armenian references are *S*
(the Sis ms.), *Q* (the questionable full-length variants), and *E* (the
epitomes).

ARMENIAN P-C, CHAPTERS 1-38; GREEK, BOOK I,
CHAPTERS 1-16

Although *P* is missing six to eight pages at the beginning of the
manuscript (Dashian, p. 139), it begins like *A, L,* and *V. A* is missing chapters 14 and 35. In the opening chapters, *P* is often closest
to *B.*

I

[1] The syntax of *P* could be read, "after whom it befell the
throne to conquer," etc. But the vocabulary is practically identical
to *A* and has been so translated. The *E* texts read, "who, after the
kingdom of Egypt, ruled through magic sorcery, and defeated all
his enemies. (*P*, p. 1, note 1)

[2] *P* agrees with *B.*

[3] *P* agrees with *B* and *V,* "ex fonte limpidissimo." *A* reads "rain
water."

[4] *P* agrees with *V,* "mox viveri ac vivere visebantur."

160

[5] *P* agrees with *V*, "deos superos inferosque." *A*: ἀγγέλους καὶ θεὸν Λιβύης Ἄμμωνα. Throughout the text, the Armenian usually states չաստուածսն (non-gods), to emphasize that pagan divinities are in question.

2

[1] *P* is corrupt. Armenian variants read էքսփրակրատորէս (ēksp'rakratorēs).

[2] The names of the nations vary greatly among the various versions, and will not be generally remarked upon in the notes.

[3] The Homeric verses appear only in *L*.

4

[1] "and . . . to leave," appear only in *A*.

[2] *P* agrees with *A* and *L*.

[3] *P* agrees with *B* and *C*.

[4] The Armenian is inconsistent in spelling almost all proper names: thus, Pelles, Pellas, and Pella. In general a standard form has been adopted in the translation.

[5] *P* agrees with *A* and *V*.

5

[1] Sinopos agrees with *A* and *L*, although the entire remark is closer in sense to *B* and *C*. This chapter is not in *V*.

6

[1] This spelling is used throughout the translation for the sake of uniformity. The text variously reads Olompiada, Olompia, etc., always spelling the name with two "o"s, as is Mount Olympos, too, in the Armenian.

[2] This nicety of protocol appears also in *A*.

7

[1] Dashian (p. 216) suggests that կամք should read կարգք.

[2] *P* has the questionable noun ամմովնագէտք (ammovnagētk'). It may not refer to the god as his name is spelled Ամոն (Amon) throughout the text. *A* reads ἀμουμάντεις which is also inexplicable. *E* variants read ամանագէտք (dish-seers).

8

[1] The Armenian transliterates many of the Greek words in its description of the horoscope.

9

[1] *P* generally parallels *B* and *C*; but Olympias is considerably more inquisitive in the Armenian.

10

[1] *ս՟արկ՟ձասկս* is meant for *սա՟ճ՟ձասկս*, as per other variants (*P*, p. 6, note 1) and Dashian (p. 216).

12

[1] *P* has only the adverb *սՐ՟ո՟ս*, while variants (*P*, p. 7, note 3) read *ս՟ո՟սս՟ ի ՟նե՟ր՟ ֊ռս ՟ ՟ի ս՟ն՟ն՟կ՟ի՟ն ի՟ս՟ո՟ս*, "access to my room."

13

[1] The Armenian translator seems to have read βασιλέα as a feminine nominative, and mistakenly translated it as *դ՟ձ՟խ՟ո՟ս*, "queen".

16

[1] T'reanç has filled the lacunae in the Armenian from an unspecified Greek text.

[2] Babylonios is one of rare instances where *P* agrees only with *C*. The name does not appear in *A*, *B*, or *V*.

[3] Stephanos of Byzantium claimed that for this reason Alexandria was called Λεοντόπολις. Müller (p. 160, note 2) states that Stephanos had in turn taken the reference from Iason Argivus.

18

[1] *A* claims that the explanation reconciled Philip to his wife's being pregnant.

21

The last sentences of 20 and 21 are not in *A*, *B*, or *C*. In general, chapters 17-22 read like *B*, *C*, and *V*. *A* is often different and lacks many passages.

24

[1] Literally: "not a little."

[2] B and C give no name; A and V read like P. Here, as in Olompiada, the Armenian seems to have kept the declension ending as part of the proper name.

25

[1] P reads literally "the time was in-between." Q variants read, "and the sun was near noon."

26

[1] ԲագակուՈ means "incomplete". Here A has much added astrological mythology. P reads like B, C, and the Valerius variant cod. 8519, fol. 7.

28

[1] This sentence appears only in A and B; but the paragraph in general is closer in sense to B.

29

[1] Dashian, p. 17, remarks that Lakrine is mentioned by the historian Arrian; she becomes the sister of Melanos from the fact that Plutarch calls her the sister of Κλεῖτος ὁ μέλας. The stem կեղտ of կեղտացի, which transliterates as kelt, means dirt or blackness. Some variants read կելտացեղ which is surely Celt (P, p. 15, note 3).

[2] Only V names Aristocles Lampsacenus.

[3] "Of Nicomitachos, the Stagirite" is not in A, B, C, or V.

[4] V alone states, "Favorini librum, qui omni genere historiae superscribitur." Dashian, p. 16, states on Zacher's authority that this is Favorinus Arelatensis, the author of histories of Trajan and Hadrian. This remark has been one of the reasons the work has been held to be no earlier than A.D. 200. The latest date the book could have been written has been set as no later than the late fourth century, since the text mentions the shrine of Sarapis in Alexandria which Theodosius destroyed in 387.

31

[1] A reads ὃι τῆς Καπποδοκίας ἄρχοντς.

163

² *C*, too, states "horse"; other texts say "colt." Here *P* parallels *B* in general.

³ Only *B* and *V* mention this comparison with Pegasus. *V* has the name Laomedontus, but in a very different context.

⁴ This remark is not in *A*, *B*, *C*, or *V*.

⁵ The syntax of this sentence is not clear. Variants of the *Q* group (*P*, p. 16, note 5) read, "Such things have happened among the Hellenes."

⁶ Greek versions read, "without a bridle".

33

¹ *Q* variant reads "for when I became an astrologer, I learned that it was written. . . ."

34

¹ *A* adds a monologue by Alexander on the equitableness of Nectanebos' fate.

35

¹ This chapter is missing in *A*.

36

¹ *A*, *B*, and *C* read διὰ μέσης τῆς πόλεως. *V* reads "medium Pellae."

37

¹ As in ch. 19, "Stagirite" appears only in the Armenian. Dashian, p. 226, suggests that it may be a later entry. Here *P* follows *B* and *V*; *C* has many additions.

ARMENIAN P-C, CHAPTERS 39-46; GREEK, BOOK I, CHAPTER 16

The eight letters that follow are not in *A*, *B*, or *C*. The Armenian differs considerably with *V* in detail; in general, *V* is briefer, lacking for example the parting salutations of the letters of chapters 39, 43, 44, and 45.

40

¹ *P* reads յայրդ վերայ. The translation is according to the variants (*P*, p. 20, note 1) which read այրդ 'ի վերայ.

44

[1] Literally: "They have done the contrary thing."

ARMENIAN P-C, CHAPTERS 47-72; GREEK, BOOK I, CHAPTERS 17-25

In this section, the Armenian generally parallels *A* and *V*; however, *A* is missing chapters 59 and 62. In chapters 68 and 69, the text is closer to *B*.

49

[1] *Q* variant has a long parenthetical description of Pisa and the festivities which were held in the stadium. *P* is corrupt and the noun "Pisa" is from *E*.

50

[1] Some Armenian variants give Melin, which could perhaps corroborate *V*, which reads "Elim."

51

[1] *P* literally reads "briny" (աղաշնր).
[2] *A* reads τοῦ ἐμοῦ πατρὸς σπορὰν καὶ μητρὸς γαστέρα ἱερὸν; this is not in *B*, *C*, or *V*.

54

[1] The first half of this saying does not appear in *V*, and the last is in neither *A*, *B*, *C*, or *V*.

55

[1] *P* is corrupt; the reading is from *Q*.
[2] As shall be frequently the case, the Greek play on words is lost in Armenian (νικάω :λαὸς) as it is in English.

56

[1] This genealogy is questionable. *P* reads զբոյրն իւր "his sister," which the editor has deleted as a mistake (*P*, p. 27, note 1). *A* reads γαμοῦντα τὴν ἀδελφὴν αὐτοῦ. Müller has corrected αὐτοῦ to read "Attalus," as does Valerius. Interestingly, a sister of Alexander by this name is mentioned again in ch. 274.

59

[1] This chapter does not appear in *A*, but is in *B*, *C*, and *V*. Its antiquity is attested to by the fact that it is a passage that Xorenaçi had incorporated into his *History*.

[2] *P* reads as translated. Dashian, p. 216, suggests *վարկին* instead of *պարկին*.

[3] *P* reads literally "they did the last things."

62

[1] This chapter does not appear in *A*, but there are varying accounts in *B*, *C*, and *V*.

63

[1] Only *C* has a chapter heading at this point. Up to this chapter, each of the Greek chapters had a title; but they cease here.

65

[1] This is not in *A* or *V*. *B* and *C* read οὐ γὰρ ὁ θέλων τοὺς Ἕλληνας εἰς δουλείαν ὑποτάσσει as part of Alexander's preceding remark.

66

[1] Here *A* and *B* have separate additions. *P* agrees with *V*.

67

[1] In the incident of Pausianos' attempted abduction of Olympias, *P* parallels *B*. *A* has many additions, and *V* is much briefer and reads quite differently in chapters 68-72.

68

[1] *P* reads "killed," but the logic of the passage indicates that the verb is a mistake here.

69

This is a literal reading of *P*. *Q* variants read *թաղեաց զհայր իւր թագաւորէն*, "and he buried his father as befits a king," which is closer to the Greek: θάπτεται οὖν βασιλικῶς.

70

[1] As usual, there is considerable discrepancy among the proper

names of the various texts. *V* omits many of them; *C* adds Thebans and Athenians; and *P* adds Thetalians and Thracians.

ARMENIAN P-C, CHAPTERS 73-102; GREEK, BOOK I, CHAPTERS 26-36

This is the most varied section in the diverse manuscripts. After Alexander collects his armies, *B* and *C* immediately go on to other subjects (Alexander's war with the Hellenes), which *A* and *V* recount later. They tell here of his going to Sicily, Italy, and Africa, the building of Alexandria, and the destruction of Tyre. These incidents are related later in *B* and *C*. All the mss. come together again in Greek I, 29 (*P*, ch. 74). Here, *P* generally reads like *A* and *V*. *B* and *C* are lacking practically all of chapters 79, 84, and 85.

73

[1] The numbers vary greatly among versions, and tally in none.

74

[1] T'reanç has chosen Մադոն from the variants. *P* reads Մոդոն (Modon), which Dashian (p. 230), suggests may be a corruption of *A*, διὰ τοῦ θερμώδοντος ποταμοῦ.

75

[1] *P* and *A* alone say it was the crown of Capitoline Zeus. Aramazd was the supreme deity of the Armenian pagan pantheon, and is the usual Armenian rendering of Zeus.

[2] *P* reads like *A*. However, Armenian variants read "Khalkedonians" as suggests the *A* codex (χαλχ . . .).

77

[1] *P* transliterates as "Pharitos." *A* reads εἰς τὴν Φαρίτιδα νῆσον.

[2] *P* transliterates as "Protiatos."

[3] This passage, as almost all of the poetry of the Greek, is rendered into prose in the Armenian. Dashian (p. 47) notes that this is a passage that recurs almost verbatim in Xorenaçi.

78

[1] Here again the word play of the Greek is lost, as it is in *V*.

79

¹ The Armenian reads Posiris, which the editor of *P* has changed to conform with the Latin and Greek (*P*, p. 37, note 1).

² The names of the villages appear only in the Armenian and *A*, with considerable divergence between the two.

³ P reads like *A*, *B*, and *C*. *V* gives 16 villages and 12 rivers.

⁴ As Dashian suggests (p. 233), the word "column" has been added as there is no noun for the genitive Արգեայն to modify. *A* reads Ἀργέου στύλος.

80

¹ The Greek reads Ἑρμούπολις and Ὁρμούπολις.

² Dashian, p. 194, suggests that the original translator read ἤπειροι for ἔμποροι of *A*.

81

¹ See ch. 79, note 1.

82

¹ Սկզբունք usually refers to an impersonal creative force, but the context suggests an agent.

² The Latin omits this play altogether, and its effect is lost in translation. (Gr: Ὑπόνομος, ὑπόνομος.)

83

¹ Only *P*, *A*, and *V* compare the sizes of the cities. They also mention Rome and Babylon and their dimensions.

² P is corrupt. The Armenian variants read, կարթաոռն or կարթական. The editor of *P*, p. 39, note 3, does not state the source of his change.

84

¹ P reads Protēs.

85

¹ Dashian, p. 216, corrects բան զթոչունք to read բան զի թոչունք; the translation is literal to *P*.

86

¹ This is the transliteration of Թարկ, which means "place of habitation." It is probably the translation of Στοά.

² Ա.զրիւրք should probably be Ա.զրիւք or "mound," as the Greek reads Κοπρία. (Dashian, p. 189.)

87

¹ The Greek pattern, A, B, Γ, Δ, E—'Αλεξάνδρος βασιλεὺς γένος διὸς ἔκτιοε (πόλιν ἀείμνηστον) has been imitated with complete success in the Armenian. *V* does not attempt the effect.

² This is an Egyptian division of the year corresponding to our January (Müller, p. 35, ch. xxxii, note 10). A, B, and C read ἰαννουαρίου·

³ The sacrifice to Alexander as belonging to the race of serpents recalls Ammon's apparition as a serpent.

88

¹ See ch. 77, note 2.

90

¹ The Armenian translator chose Anahit, the supreme goddess of the Armenian pagan pantheon, to translate Hera.

93

¹ This whole reply is in badly corrupt poetic form in *A* and appears as verse in *V* also.

² *V* sees the elements as propitious.

³ Dashian, p. 235, cites this as an interesting example of a repetition in the Armenian text where the first account parallels *A* and the second is closer to *B*, which, however, is much briefer.

⁴ The riddle is solved of course by substituting the letter equivalents of the Greek numbers, which gives Sarapis.

94

¹ The Zoroastrian deity Zrowan is equated with Kronos.

97

¹ *P* is corrupt; the translation is suggested by Dashian, pp. 219-20, and agrees with the Greek.

99

¹ Dashian, pp. 60-63, draws lengthy parallels between the account by Xorenaçi of the siege of Tigranakert and that of Tyre

to show that the surviving text is largely true to the fifth-century translation and, also, to support the claim of Xorenaçi's authorship.

[1] The Greek play is on Τύρος and τυρός.

ARMENIAN P-C, CHAPTERS 103-19; GREEK, BOOK I, CHAPTERS 37-42

In this first section on the battles of Alexander and Darius, the Armenian equals A and V, in general. However, A is missing ch. 117.

[1] This is the Armenian name for Mithras.

[1] The reference to Tyre is not in A, B, C, or V.

[1] P reads Ել զԱսորիս եւ բնաւ Հնագանդեայան, which Dashian, p. 236, regards as a printing error. Translation is per P.

[1] The proper names appear only in A and V. In Armenian, Hystaspes is Vštasp.

[2] A gives no number; V reads "five."

[1] This passage is very faulty in the Armenian, as was observed by Dashian, p. 236.

[1] A reads Τινάργῳ; B and C give Πινάριῳ.

[2] Six Armenian variants read "ruler-less".

[3] պարծեցին has been translated as պարծեցիս to smooth a generally very questionable passage.

[1] Chapters 113 and 114 follow A, but are not in B or C. V is less detailed than P and A. Here B and C give a long aside on

Darius' forces, Alexander's crossing the Tanros, and his bathing in the Cydnos, which *A* and *V* have in the second book.

114

[1] The translation is according to *P*. Dashian, p. 216, suggests that *զպարոց* was a mistake for *զպարից*, which would parallel *A* τῶν Περσῶν.

115

[1] Arrian, Curtius, and Plutarch name Ἀντιοχεύς according to Müller (p. 46, note 22).

116

[1] This translation is suggested by Dashian, p. 217, who reads *առաւել բաշութեամբ վարել* instead of *առաւել բաշութիւն*.

117

[1] This seems to be a repetition of the same number and does not agree with *B*, *C*, or *V*.

119

[1] This corroborates codex Σκαμάνδρῳ and *V*, which Maius had corrected to "Cassandro." (Müller, p. 47, ch. XLII, note 4.)

ARMENIAN P-C, CHAPTERS 120-34; GREEK, BOOK I, CHAPTERS 42-57

This section deals with Alexander's wars with the Greeks and Thebans. *A* is missing a page at the beginning of this section and thus starts at about ch. 124. There is a big difference among versions starting about ch. 125. From this point (Gr. Bk. I, ch. 45) to ch. 148 (Gr. Bk. II, ch. 6), *A*, *V*, and *P* differ from *B* and *C*, which recount this material elsewhere and somewhat differently. *P* in general follows *A* and *V*.

120

[1] "Keraton" is not in the Greek. *V* reads "Summo in culmine Tauri montis." Dashian, p. 196, suggests that the Armenian might have had a Greek word such as κεράτιον to translate and rendered it as a proper name.

171

¹ All the Armenian variants read **Պերիս** (Peris) which the editor of *P* changed to conform with the context below.

¹ In this paragraph, *P* often parallels only *B*; such an instance is the word "ἐπταβόειον".

² From this point through ch. 124, there is a lacuna in all the Armenian full-length versions. The fact that they existed originally is attested to by other ancient Armenian sources which Dashian cites on p. 176. This passage is also cited by Dashian, p. 140, to show that all the full-length versions were based on the same lost original.

The entire bracketed section is translated by the editor of *P* from the Greek, and the subordinate parenthetical passages are from Valerius. The editor does not specify which texts he was working from.

Kroll too quotes extensively from Valerius in this passage as *A* is extremely corrupt also.

The Armenian epitomes read as follows (*P*, pp. 60-61, note 5):

"And having dined with the mother of Darius, he went to Macedon with the slaves he had taken from Darius. And he traveled to Abder. And the Abderians locked the gates. Alexander ordered that they be set afire. And they sent him their entreaties that 'we have not done so as enemies, but because we are afraid of Darius. For after you leave, he will come and devastate our city. For we serve the strongest man. If you defeat Darius, we shall be your slaves.' And the king was amazed at their cleverness and went on past there to Boeotia and he devastated all of Olynthos and likewise the cities of the Chaldeans. And he left with his troops and stayed near the Euxinos River, and he subjugated everyone. And he sacrificed to the female statue and went on. And he came upon the winter season there; and there was a terrible famine among the soldiers and in the lands. And he ordered horses slain and eaten, so that they not die of hunger. And they stayed alive in that fashion. For he said, 'If a man stay alive, it is possible to find the things he needs, both horses and goods; but after he dies, horses are worthless.' And from there he came to the Lokrians, etc."

The *Q* variants read as follows:

"And having dined with the mother of Darius, he sailed to

Macedon with the slaves he had taken in the war with Darius. And he left all the slaves there and went back to the land of the Arabians, and he traveled straight to the city of Abder. And the Abderians closed their gates to him and did not allow him to enter. And Alexander got angry and ordered the city burnt. And they sent a legate to him and they said, 'We did not close the gates in scorn of you, but we are afraid of Darius. If his rule remain unshaken, then he will afterwards harm us because of our receiving you. But if you forcibly open them, we will obey the mighty emperor, be it you or Darius.' And when Alexander heard this, he said, 'If this is the reason you closed them, then go and open them, and remain in peace. For now I shall not enter your city until I have slain Darius. And then you shall obey me.' "

125

[1] P reads like A and V. The existence of this form in the fifth-century Armenian text indicates that if this is a copy error as suggested by Müller, p. 49, ch. XLV, note 1, then it existed already in the Greek prior to the fifth century.

[2] P is faulty and has been corrected per above and V. Other variants read Ֆիրոս, "Phœbus," P, p. 60, note 2, which is perhaps a corruption of the Greek Φοιβολάλον.

127

[1] The Armenian full-length copies give the details of the destruction of Thebes in ch. 132. The epitomes and Q place them here, as does V.

The epitomes read: "(And he ordered) the gates be set afire. First to be stricken and razed was the gate they call the Cadmean, on which Alexander was standing. And then they seized the king. A few men rushed through the opening alone and harassed and turned many men to flight. And in three days, they destroyed the whole city. And they fired upon those who were on the walls, which they destroyed from the base; and they put all the inhabitants to death with their swords. And countless men were piled upon one another. For Alexander had ordered that all be done rapidly to the point that they grew tired; for the swords had been given so much blood to drink. And a certain Ismenias, etc."

Q variants read: "And in three days the city was burnt by fire. But first the gate upon which Alexander was standing was set afire. And the king himself rushed through a small opening alone. And many Thebans, upon seeing him, turned and fled. And other troops entered through the gates. In the city there were 4,000 soldiers, and they were all slain. And the city was razed from its foundations and set ablaze. For upon orders from Alexander, the Macedonians easily accomplished what they wanted to. And in the city, there was a learned lutist by the name of Ismenias, etc."

129

[1] *A* is so faulty in this recital that Müller, p. 51, note 23, states, "Quod sequitur carmen lacerum sine meliorum codicum ope restitui nequit." As Dashian, p. 238, observes, the Armenian, too, in rendering in prose the Greek poetry, has become a conglomeration of ambiguities. *V* is much shortened.

[2] *P* reads 'ի նաւ վազել, "running to a ship." Dashian corrects this to parallel the Greek.

[3] Dashian suggests that with a slight change, this could read բարշեցելոյ Դերկեայ, "of Dirce who was dragged about."

[4] This is Dashian's, p. 217, suggested correction of *P*'s Մեփիքս.

131

[1] This transliteration of բիովտեան suggests perhaps the Bacchic rites held in this region, and thus the reeds of Dionysius.

132

[1] The Armenian seems to have confused Ἰσμηνός and Ἰσμηνίας.

[2] "անքաղաք" is the Armenian of "ἄπολεις."

133

[1] The Armenian texts read Ալկիդես, which the editor had corrected to agree with the following chapter and *V*.

[2] The adjective պարապամարտ is formed from ἱμαντόμαχος. However, the Armenian has the literal sense of one who fights upon the walls of a city, and it is in this sense that Magistros has used the adjective in reference to Achilles (Dashian, p. 32).

134

[1] The *P* text says only մրցումն; and though it does not has used the adjective in reference to Achilles (Dashian, p. 32). translate πάλην, παγκράτιον καὶ πυγμήν.

² This is evidently faulty for Polydeuces, as below.

³ Here *A* and *V* start the second book. The Armenian alone attributes the first part of the work to Aristotle.

ARMENIAN P-C, CHAPTERS 135-49; GREEK, BOOK II, CHAPTERS 1-6

135

¹ *P* reads "*կորէ*", the transliteration of Κόρη, by which name Proserpine was worshiped in Attica. In ch. cxxxvi, the author translates the word to *աղջիկ*.

139

¹ Dashian, p. 196, suggests that the Armenian made a proper name of πρότερος.

140

¹ *P* transliterates as "Eskines"; the Greek is Αἰσχίνης.

² The Greek reads: τί τὸ βράδος τῆς βουλῆς.

141

¹ Dashian, p. 215, says that the text should be properly punctuated to read: "Are we now afraid to fight with Alexander?" Aeschines says, "Alexander, etc."

² The Armenian alone compliments Darius in this passage and below (cxxxii). The name *Պիւրեայ*, which transliterates "Piwreus," is not in the Greek or *V*.

³ The Armenian variants read *Մնեսիքերբայ*, *Ձնեսիքերբայ* or *Նեսիքերբայ*. *V* reads "Mnesicharmus." The editor of *P* has corrected the text to conform with the retort below.

142

¹ The punctuation of *P* has been changed for sense and fluency. The Armenian sentence stops after "citizen".

² The Latin, too, does not attribute the victory to the wisdom of the Greeks. In general, the Armenian seems least willing to denigrate Xerxes.

143

¹ *V* supports this: "adclamatio. . . . Amphictyonum erat."

175

144

[1] This is an obvious reference to Alexander but there is no clarification in the text.

[2] "ршն գшմ՛ննшյն" has been translated as "ршնդի шմ՛ննшյն."

[3] The Armenian corresponds literally to the Greek: τὴν τοῦ Ἄρεως τόλμην καθοπλίζεσθαι.

146

[1] This is the form of the name "Cyrus" that is customary in classical Armenian from the Assyrian translations. (Dashian, p. 189.)

[2] P reads "Alcipiades," which has been corrected according to the Greek.

148

[1] The translation is according to P. Dashian, p. 217, suggests that щшнմ՛ուֆ՛ին should be read as գшщшшршшшուֆ՛ին, "preparation."

[2] "կшմ՛ш" has a questionable sense here. Dashian, p. 217, suggests "фшռս", "glory."

149

[1] Alexander's reproach to this entreaty, which appears in the Greek and Latin, is missing from the Armenian.

ARMENIAN P-C, CHAPTERS 150-74; GREEK, BOOK II, CHAPTERS 7-13

These chapters deal with Alexander's expedition against Darius, up to the point where he goes to him in disguise as his own messenger. P generally reads like A and V; but ch. 159 appears only in P and A.

150

[1] A, B, C, and V meet again at this point in the text. The Armenian seems to be the most complete in this chapter, as this sentence, from "lest" to "country," is not in A, but is in B and C.

[2] This last sentence appears only in V and P.

151

[1] The Armenian resembles B and C. A reads Ὀξυάθρης; V gives "Oxyathrus."

152

¹ "*Մի֊ջագետաց*" is the literal Armenian translation of "Meso-potamians."

² "*Շամիրամ*" is the Armenian of Semiramus.

153

¹ *V* also attributes this speech to another satrap, while the Greek gives it to Darius.

154

¹ *P* reads like *A* and *B*. Müller suggests "Cydnum" from Valerius.

² *V* reads "una cum armis." *P* agrees with the Greek.

155

¹ All Greek variants start with "D". Armenian "*Գ*" and "*Բ*", could have been easily confused; but the spelling is consistent throughout.

158

¹ This is a tributary of the Euphrates in Armenia. The text is inconsistent as the following line reads *Եփրատ*. Cf. ch. cxxxv, note 1.

² Dashian, p. 43, notes that this is a very exact local description and was quoted by Sebēos, a contemporary of Xorenaçi.

159

¹ This is the Armenian name for the Tigris from biblical translations. (Dashian, p. 189.)

² This passage, much shortened, exists only as a marginal note on codex *A*, and does not appear in *B*, *C*, or *V*.

162

¹ This Turkish form of Alexander's name is of unexplained provenance in the text. (Dashian, p. 142.)

165

¹ The Armenian uses this faulty transliteration of ῎αγκυρα as a proper name. Thus the sense of the Greek is very different.

² *Q* variants read: ". . . that you treated my family well. Now if you were willing to act properly and win my love, you would

come to me; and I would give you godly honors because of the honor you have done my family."

166

¹ Q variants read: "I have been accustomed to treat everyone well, and have treated your family in the same way, for they have fallen from heaven to earth."

169

¹ A reads "Κοβάρξην".

171

¹ P reads *երկբայութեամբ*, which literally means "with un-certitude".

172

¹ P reads as *A*. This is not in *B*, *C*, or *V*.

173

¹ Dashian, p. 82, notes that the tenth-century historian Łazar Pʻarpeçi states also that Alexander used lights as well as boughs. This is not in *A* or *V*; but it is mentioned in *B* and *C* that he had torches tied upon the animals. This must have fallen from the Armenian text at a very old date as the epitomes read: "Sharp-witted Alexander seized many goats and lighting many torches onto the horses at night, showed them off from afar. And thus the onlookers had the impression that they were vast armies. And by day he took the flocks that were grazing there, and cutting boughs from the trees and pines, tied them on the quadrupeds." (*P*, p. 96, note 1.)

ARMENIAN P-C, CHAPTERS 175-208; GREEK, BOOK II, CHAPTERS 14-22

This section tells of Alexander's going to Darius disguised as a messenger, his final victory over the Persian king, and his conquest of the East. *P* reads like *A*, *B*, *C*, and *V*. But in one important passage of two pages at the end of ch. 199, it parallels only *A*.

176

¹ Neither this chapter heading nor the preceding one appears

in *A*, *B*, *C*, or *V*. But Dashian, p. 99, states that the language of the former bears evidence of antiquity.

[2] *P* reads like *V*. *A*, *B*, and *C* name Bucephalus.

177

[1] This is a transliteration of Ս*Ŀ*ų*ш*ш*ш*ն*ն, the meaning of which is uncertain. (Dashian, p. 207, note 1.)

179

[1] This is the city of Susa.

180

[1] The syntax indicates that the printed text is probably wrong and that the subject of the verbs must be Parasanges of the following sentence. Thus the paragraphing would be wrong. (Dashian, pp. 215-16, note 1.) The translation has changed the verbs to passives to keep the form of *P*.

181

[1] Here *P* reads like *B* and *C*.

182

[1] This is an instance where *P* resembles only *C*.

187

[1] This and the following chapters are rich in detail in the Armenian. Dashian, p. 190, considers this as perhaps a rare example of the translator's amplification of the original text.

190

[1] This passage is very faulty in the Armenian.

191

[1] This is not in *A* or *C*, but does appear in *B* and *P*. Previous chapters have shown the nuances of this epistolatory protocol.

192

[1] The parenthetical lines are missing from all Armenian copies, and have been translated by the editor of *P* from an unspecified Greek text (p. 108, note 2). Dashian, p. 141, cites this lacuna along

179

with that of chapters 122-23 to show that identical gaps in all extant full-length mss. indicate that they are all based on one lost original.

193

[1] P reads Հարուստ which literally means "rich" or "mighty." Dashian, p. 192, thinks that the word is used here in the place of Հետևակ, a "follower" or "infantryman."

195

[1] This is the Armenian form of Ariobarzanes.

[2] P parallels B and C; this is not in A or V.

197

[1] The Armenian has Darius disavow the Persians. This is not in A, B, C, or V, yet seems to sustain the thought that immediately follows. It is not however confirmed by Alexander's actions in the following paragraph.

198

[1] The Armenian uses the Arabic word "Թապուտ".

199

[1] Such was the official Persian designation of Persians and non-Persians.

[2] This chapter is rife with difficulties in the Armenian, but in content it generally reads as A.

203

[1] This name is taken from the Greek by the editor of P. P reads Aroulites; other variants give Aroulitos. There is no name in V.

205

[1] Dashian, p. 213, cites this letter to show another instance where the Armenian surprisingly parallels in one passage A and immediately afterwards coincides with B. Thus, "Now we wrote. . . . Anahit" reads like A.

[2] "And . . . marriage" follows B.

208

[1] Karanon appears as an unintelligible common noun in P, with the adjective "Macedonian."

² According to Dashian, this is a corruption of Nemesis and Dike (p. 288).

³ At this point, Book II of *A* and *V* comes to an end. The Armenian continues as before without any break.

ARMENIAN P-C, CHAPTER 209; GREEK, BOOK II, CHAPTERS 23-43

This important letter from Alexander to his mother and his teacher Aristotle is not in *A* and *V* but only in *B*, *C*, and *L*, where it has been much elaborated. *C* recounts the incidents in the third person.

209

¹ This is the transliteration of *Այծս* ("*goats*"), which probably renders the Greek 'Αιγάς.

² Dashian, p. 196, observes that the translator of *P* has probably made the name Kattison from the Greek κατὰ 'Ισσόν.

³ This is the transliteration of the Armenian *անամկսիրսոն*, which in turn seems to be the corrupted transliteration of an unidentified Greek word.

⁴ *P* reads *մաղկայ*. A change of "*դ*" to "*ղ*" would give a resemblance to the Greek Μαλακοῦ.

⁵ *P* resembles *C* ἀναφνήτων, for *B* reads ἀνάφαντον.

⁶ This is the translation of *անկածորք*.

⁷ The editor of *P* has corrected the text which reads *ովքրորք*.

⁸ *P* is faulty. The reading is from the *S* variant (*P*, p. 124, note 4).

⁹ Dashian, p. 196, suggests that the name might be a corruption of *B* ἐἰς τὰς πατρίδας.

¹⁰ The Armenian is the transliteration of *B* δάνδηκες.

¹¹ "*դերերի*" means "hydnum." (Dashian, p. 83.)

¹² *P* is defective. The Armenian epitomes read *լոյս անցանել*, "to pass a light", which was the choice of the editor of *P*. The translation, however, is according to the text of Tovma Arcrowni, '*ի լոյս անցանել 'ի նաւէն* (*P*, p. 127, note 3). Arcrowni's lengthy citation from this passage and its similarity to the Armenian *P-C* is cited by Dashian, pp. 35-38, to once again demonstrate the fidelity of the existing text to the fifth-century original translation.

¹ Here *A*, *B*, *C*, and *V* start Book III.

ARMENIAN P-C, CHAPTERS 210-23; GREEK, BOOK III, CHAPTERS 1-15

Like the Greek and Latin versions, *P* starts the campaign against Poros at this point. The visit to the gymnosophists follows. There is much variation in the accounts, and *A* and *V* have additional chapters. Here *P* generally follows *B* and *C*.

215

¹ This passage is not in *A*. Only *C* states θεωρήσασ γὰρ τὸ ξένον τῶν θηρίων ἐθαύμασεν; then *B* and *C* continue ἀνθρώποις γὰρ εἶχεν ἔθος μάχεσθαι, οὐ θηρίοις.

221

¹ *P* has the literal translation ⟨Armenian⟩, "naked philosophers."

223

¹ In this chapter, the Armenian is more detailed than any of the other texts, even Valerius, which it is closest to. Certain passages seem to bear the imprint of a Christian scribe.

ARMENIAN P-C, CHAPTER 224; GREEK, BOOK III, CHAPTERS 16-17

This long letter of Alexander to Aristotle is found only in *A* and *V*, in this position and in this form.

224

¹ In *A* there is a separate chapter heading for the letter; while in *B* and *C*, it is interwoven into the narrative of the text, with no indication of its being a letter. *B* and *C* have 18 pages of digressions on the marvels of India.

² The editor of *P* has taken the name from *V*. Armenian variants read: Parasias, Parsias, or Parskakan.

³ *A* and *V* name the beast Hebdomadorion. Only *V* mentions "elephantos."

⁴ The hours are questionable. The text seems to suggest that

182

night fell at four o'clock, the army marched until nine, dined, and then slept until daybreak at four.

⁵ *V* reads: "arundinibus quae ad triginta cubitorum spatia supercrescerent. Crassitudo vero earum supra eam quanta est hominis crassitudo." *A* says πηχῶν δ' περίμετρον ἔχοντες·

⁶ The translation is from the variants 'ի չափ կանդնոյ, which agrees with *A* and *V*. *P* reads կանդունք.

⁷ This is not in *A*. *V* reads "Odontotyrannus."

⁸ *P* reads բունութիւն which Dashian, p. 194, note 4, considers a printing error. The translation parallels *A* κατὰ φύσιν.

⁹ This was the first month of the Armenian year. It is the equivalent of August of the Julian calendar. *A* reads μηνιαίᾳ τρίτῃ.

¹⁰ *A* gives μυροβαλάνος, which is a sweet acorn or date tree.

¹¹ *B* reads μονθεὰ μαθόυς; *A*, μονθοῦ ἐμαοῦσαι.

¹² *P* here follows *B*.

¹³ The words "ouzomores" and "ioulidas" are unknown, as they have been lost in the Greek.

¹⁴ զղաւկ is the transliteration of γλαυκ. Dashian says it is a kind of fish, but the sense suggests the color.

¹⁵ This is the Armenian name for Semiramis.

ARMENIAN P-C, CHAPTERS 225-50, GREEK, BOOK III, CHAPTERS 18-24

These are the incidents pertaining to Candace and Semiramis; Alexander's disguised visit to her and her splendid palace; generally. *P* reads as *A*.

226

¹ *V* reads: "rectius tibi facturae si veneris, etc." The Greek versions read εἰ δὴ μὴ βούλεσθε ἔρχεσθαι.

227

¹ As in the Greek, this passage is quite corrupt in the Armenian.

229

¹ No doubt Ptolemaeus Soter.

238

¹ *P* reads եղբայրն, nom. s., in apparent reference to Alexander. The Greek reads: συνεσθίων τοῖς ἀδελθοῖς Κανδαύλου.

[1] The name varies in all the texts.

[2] P transliterates "Karabos"; this name should no doubt be Կարբագոս, as in chapter 244 and V.

[1] The Armenian variants read: "and yet you are now acting most foolishly. Now what can you do to prevent their fighting?"

[1] The last part of this chapter through ch. 249, "Sesonchousis said:", is not in A or C. V is quite different and lacks the names of the cities.

ARMENIAN P-C, CHAPTERS 251-60; GREEK, BOOK III, CHAPTERS 25-30

This includes the correspondence with the Amazons, the letter to Olympias concerning his travels, and the episode in Babylon. Chapters 255-57 are only in V. The beginning of Olympias' letter is only in A and V.

[1] V reads "si quidem te coronamus corona aurea annua quae sit ponderis quando tu iusseris". A and C read Στεφανοῦμεν δὲ σε κατ᾽ ἐνιαυτὸν ὅσον ἂν συντάξῃς.

[1] P agrees with only V in this chapter through 257. V gives the name Prasiacam. Dashian, p. 199, suggests that the Greek παρασάγγας had been misread as the name of a place.

[1] Odysseus and Nestor are mentioned only in the Armenian.

[1] Here A, B, C, and V reunite.
[2] P agrees with V. A says ἐν ἡμέραις κέ.
[3] A reads τὸ μεν ὕφος πηχῶν ιγ᾽ τὸ δὲ πλάτος πηχῶν β᾽. V has

"altitudo . . . cubitis . . . quindecim, crassitudo vero in cubitis duobus."

4 P transliterates "mtłal," which appears only in the Armenian. Variants read *մսխալ*, "msxal."

5 As in ch. 109, the Armenian again insists on "headless," which is not in *A* or *B* but in *C* and *V*. This is attested to also in a passage of the *Geography* attributed to Xorenaçi. (Dashian, pp. 80-81.)

6 *Արեգ* means "sun." The Greek reads πόλιν τοῦ ἡλίου.

7 Dashian, p. 141, note 3, sees this city of bronze as a very old Armenian addition.

8 P reads like *C*. *A* and *B* have "seven."

9 Dashian, p. 141, note 3, corrects this corrupt passage to parallel exactly *A* by the addition of two letters. *P* has meaningless common noun "gaucos."

ARMENIAN P-C, CHAPTERS 261-71; GREEK, BOOK III, CHAPTERS 31 AND 32

The circumstances are of Alexander's poisoning. The manuscripts are quite corrupt: *A* lacks large sections; *B* and *C* are much added to; and chapters 266 to 268 are only in *P* and *A*.

260

1 P reads literally "table-mate."

261

1 P is questionable in this sentence.

2 The Armenian words "*յանրաւ գամաք*" seem to be a translation of Ἤπειρος.

3 *դեղաման* probably derives from *դեղումն*, which would read like *A* χηλή. The Armenian usually has the sense of the ridge of a mouth, or any projecting cover.

262

1 The Greek gives Μῆδιος, which corroborates the reading of ch. 264.

266

1 The poisoning episode is especially important as it is very brief in *B* and *C* and very corrupt in *A*. It does not appear at all in *V*.

[1] *P* reads "they took things out".

[1] *A* has a separate title for the will.

ARMENIAN P-C, CHAPTERS 272-74; GREEK, BOOK III, CHAPTER 33

Alexander's will is not in *B* or *C*. It appears very differently in *A* and *V*. *A*, like the Armenian, is quite corrupt; *V* is greatly abridged.

[1] This is the transliteration of *Թէհուկացընց*. Dashian, p. 264, suggests that this might be a corruption of *Թէ հոռոմացընց կամք իցեն*, which would parallel the Greek.

[1] Here *P* reads like *V* in an apparent contradiction of the previously mentioned legacy to Perdikkas.

[2] *P* agrees with *V*.

[3] *ի լիւրիս* could easily have been Illyria.

[4] The *E* continue as *L*: "This will was made and sealed. And he tearfully wrote to his mother as follows. 'O Olympias, daughter of the king of Thebes, my sweet and much-missed mother. I am writing this last letter with tears and heart-felt sobs. For I remember your sweet motherly compassion, and my death seems more bitter to me because of the memory of love in my sorely wounded heart. For I depart from you with deep regret; and I deem true the words of Nectanebos, that no one can overcome his destiny. So too was I not able to flee from my fate. Now, venerable mother of mine, gather together the women chanters and lament Alexander, the pitiful, short-lived son of yours. For if death had not overtaken me, I was planning to rule the entire universe; and because of me you would have been called the mother of a world conqueror. But my greatness is lost in death; and your peripatetic and independent life has been changed. And happiness and joy and glory have been removed from our midsts. Fare thee well, for the sake of the son whom you have not seen and will never see again.' And Olympias received the letter and arranged great lamentation for the noble spirit of her son Alexander."

ARMENIAN P-C, CHAPTERS 275-84; GREEK, BOOK III, CHAPTERS 34-35

These final chapters deal with the death of Alexander. *A* is missing chapters 275-84. *B*, *C*, and *V* have additions, but omit 275-76.

277

[1] The *E* variants continue: "And he had his shroud tied on the end of a stick and had it taken all around Babylon with the announcement that of his entire treasure, Alexander, who had ruled the three ends of the earth, is taking with him this sheet alone."

281

[1] The dramatic series of verbs beginning with "ի" have been rendered by corresponding nouns.

282

[1] *P* transliterates "Niea."

283

[1] This entire chapter is from the Armenian *E*, as it is missing from all full-length versions.

[2] This seems to be the transliteration of νησιωτικὸν.

[3] This must be the transliteration of an unidentified Greek word. It is not in *A* or *V*.

284

[1] *A* has placed from here to the end of the paragraph in Alexander's will, as has *V*.

[2] տարթորակա́ն is probably a corruption of տարեւորակա́ն, which would parallel λαμβάνων ἐνιαύσιον ταλοντον.

285

[1] Dashian suggests that զընդրանիկա́յ should be զընդ Գրանիկա́յ which would read like *V* "apud Granicum".

286

[1] *B* and *C* continue with various additions. *V* and *A* end without the formal conclusion of *P*.

187

BIBLIOGRAPHY

Abel, A. *Le Roman d'Alexandre, Légendaire Médiéval.* Brussels, 1955.

Akinian, N. "Die handschriftliche Überlieferung der armenischen Übersetzung des Alexanderromans von Pseudo-Kallisthenes," *Byzantion,* Vol. XIII (1938).

Alishan, L. [Sisvan] Սիսուան. Venice, 1885. In Armenian.

Arcrowni, T. [The History of the Arcrowni Dynasty] Պատմութիւն Տանն Արծրունեաց. St. Petersburg, 1887. In Armenian.

Ausfeld, A. *Der griechische Alexanderroman.* Leipzig, 1907.

Baumgartner, A. "Über das Buch die Chrie," *Zeitschrift der deutschen morgenländischen Gesellschaft,* XL (1886), 457-515.

Berzunga, J. *Alexander the Great and the Alexander Romances.* Privately printed, 1939.

Biwzandaçi. [Kñasēr] Քննասէր. 2 vols. Stockholm, 1887. In Armenian.

Budge, E. A. Wallis. *The Alexander Book in Ethiopia.* London, 1933.

———.*The Life and Exploits of Alexander the Great.* London, 1896.

Cary, G. *The Medieval Alexander.* Cambridge, England, 1956.

Dashian, J. [Studies on Pseudo-Callisthenes' Life of Alexander] Ուսումնասիրութիւնք Առոյն. Կալիսթենեայ վարուց Աղեքսանդրի. Vienna, 1892. In Armenian.

Dowrian, E. [Ancient Armenian Religion] Հայոց Հին Կրօնը. Jerusalem, 1933. In Armenian.

Feydit, F. "La haute signification de l'invention de l'alphabet arménien par Saint Mesrop," *Pazmaveb,* IX-XII (1962) 283-89.

Gildemeister, H. "Pseudocallisthenes bei Moses von Khoren," *Zeitschrift der deutschen morgenländischen Gesellschaft,* XL (1886), 88-91.

Kroll, W. *Historia Alexander Magni.* Berlin, 1926.

Magoun, F. P., Jr. *The Gests of King Alexander of Macedon.* Cambridge, Mass., 1929.

Malxasian, S. [The Armenian History of Movses Xorenaçi] Ս*ովսէս Խորենացի Հայոց Պատմութիւն.* Erevan, 1961. In Armenian.

Meillet, A. *Altarmenisches Elementarbuch.* Heidelberg, 1913.

Merkelbach, L. "Die Quellen des griechischen Alexanderromans," *Zetemata.* Vol. IX. Munich, 1954.

Meuzel, H. "Pseudo-Callisthenes, nach der Leidener Handschrift herausgegeben," *Jahrbuch für classiche Philologie,* Neue Folge. Supplement V. Leipzig, 1871.

Meyer, P. *Alexandre le Grand dans la littérature française du moyen âge.* 2 vols. Paris, 1886.

Müller, C. *Reliqua Arriani, et Scriptorum de rebus Alexandri Magni fragmenta; Pseudo-Callisthenis Historiam Fabulosam, Itinerarium Alexandri.* Paris, 1846.

Neumann, G. *Gelehrte Anzeigen, herausg. von Mitgleidern der k. bayer. Akademie der Wissenschaften,* December, 1884, pp. 961-83.

Nöldeke, Th. "Beiträge zur Geschichte des Alexanderromans," *Denkschriften der Kaiserlichen Akademie der Wissenschaften in Wien,* XXVIII (Vienna, 1890), i.

P'arpeçi, Ł. [Letters] *Թուղթ.* Venice, 1873. In Armenian.

Pfister, F. *Der Alexanderroman des Archipresbyters Leo.* Heidelberg, 1913.

Raabe, R. Ἱστορία Ἀλεξάνδρου: *Die armenische Übersetzung der sagenhaften Alexander Biographie (P-C) auf ihre mutmassliche Grundlage zurückgeführt.* Leipzig, 1896.

Robinson, C. A., Jr. *Alexander the Great.* New York, 1947.

Tarn, W. W. *Alexander the Great.* 2 vols. Cambridge, England, 1948.

Tcheraz, M. "La légende d'Alexandre le Grand chez les Arméniens," *Revue de l'histoire des religions,* XLIII-XLIV (1901), 345-51.

T'reanç, R., ed. [The History of Alexander of Macedon] *Պատմութիւն Աղեքսանդրի Մակեդոնացւոյ.* Venice, 1842. In Armenian.

Zacher, J. *Pseudo-Callisthenes, Forschungen zur Kritik und Geschichte der ältesten Aufzeichnung der Alexandersage.* Halle, 1868.

INDEX

191